POETRY
OF THE
WORLD WARS

Edited by

MICHAEL FOSS

PETER BEDRICK BOOKS

NEW YORK

Poetry of the World Wars Copyright © 1990 by Michael O'Mara Books
All rights reserved.

First published by Peter Bedrick Books 1990
by arrangement with Michael O'Mara Books, London

Peter Bedrick Books, Inc.
2112 Broadway New York, NY 10023

Library of Congress Cataloging-in-Publication Data

Poetry of the world wars/edited by Michael Foss.— 1st American ed.
    p.   cm.

ISBN 0-87226-336-3

1. World War, 1939–1945 Poetry. 2. World War, 1914–1918 Poetry.
3. War poetry, English. 4. War poetry, American.
5. English poetry—20th century. 6. American poetry—20th century.
I. Foss, Michael.

PR1195.W66P66   1990
821'.91080358—dc20

89-18570
CIP

ISBN 0-87226-336-3

Designed by James Campus

Manufactured in Great Britain

10 9 8 7 6 5 4 3 2 1

CONTENTS

INTRODUCTION

'I had not thought death had undone so many.'

T.S. Eliot, *The Waste Land* (1922)

When the Great War began, in 1914, the mainstream of English poetry was running placidly. The bombs and shells and mustard-gas, which lacerated and devoured the youth of Europe, also shattered that complacent poetic calm.

The experience of 'total war', stalled in the Flanders mud and fed by vast, unprepared conscript armies, shocked young poets-in-uniform into a new voice. War poetry in former times had been largely celebratory, an exercise in patriotism written by non-combatants who saw fighting as an occasion for courage, endurance, comradeship and altruism. The poets of the First World War, suffering under the shadow of death, also appreciated these virtues most keenly – none more so; but they were adamant that the cause of heroism did not license the shambles of war. The blood, ordure and agony of the trenches awakened soldier-poets to both horror and responsibility. As W.B. Yeats wrote about another time of death and rebellion: 'A terrible beauty was born.'

Since the Great War was grossly inhuman, grossly cruel and grossly bungled, the reaction of the young poets was understandably extreme. The futility of the monstrous destruction forced them into the service of ordinary humanity. The need to confront (as Siegfried Sassoon put it) 'the political errors and insincerities for which the fighting men are being sacrificed' turned poetic amateurs and pretty rhymesters such as Sassoon and Wilfred Owen into fine poets and unflinching witnesses for the truth. And it was their extremity of passion that made their poems so rich and affecting. Whether it was Owen's sense of grief and pity, or Sassoon's bitter satirical disgust, or Isaac Rosenberg's tenderness amid a vision of hell, all these poets (and many less well-known names besides) tried to speak for mankind in general. They strove for universality, which was both the strength and slight weakness of their poetry. They enlivened the language and extended the sensibility of English verse. But they were myth-makers too. They were attempting to redefine war, and in doing so to exorcise it. Their experience was at the same time too painful and too absolute.

In the social and political malaise of the inter-war years, when quietism and appeasement reigned, war became unthinkable. And so, when fighting began again in 1939, poets were unsure what to say. Yet, because of the powerful success of the Great War poets, a certain kind of production was expected. The petulant demagogues who hold forth on the leader-pages demanded to know 'Where are our War Poets?' They were there, sure enough. Alun Lewis, who in 1944 died in an Indian field hospital from an accidental pistol wound, published his first collection in 1942, and others like Keith Douglas, Sidney Keyes and Roy Fuller were not far behind.

But the poetic attitudes of 1914–18 were obviously not appropriate. The message of the First World War had been thoroughly learnt and there was no need to repeat it. 'To trust anyone,' Keith Douglas wrote, 'or to admit any hope of a better world is criminally foolish, as foolish as it is to stop working for it. It sounds silly to say work without hope, but it can be done.' And, in the main, that is what the poets did; for though death in the desert was as final as death in the trenches, the war against Hitler had a kind of moral necessity that was not apparent in the earlier blind folly on the Western Front.

So, in general, the poets of the Second World War, seeing no integrity in slogans and little hope in institutions, worked a private vein of poetry. They had no universal message for mankind. It was not easy to say the grand things any more. Even in warfare there are infinite shades of grey. Afflicted as is usual in war by waste and pain and death, very often the poets preferred to turn aside and speak of a personal loss, a love suspended, a damaged ordinary life, or of boredom, discomfort, fear and puzzlement in distant lands. As a result their work was more varied and experimental than that of the First World War, and this variety was intensified by the arrival of the Americans on to the scene. Randall Jarrell, Louis Simpson, Howard Nemerov, the almost unknown Lincoln Kirstein, and several others, were strong poetic voices. They had to confront not only war (a business little known to Americans since the days of their own Civil War), but also their European past, the traditions of their fathers, and the history of their nationality in pre-American times. The American experience of the Second World War, beside being an introduction to horror, led to a questioning of identity and an examination of a cultural past.

Some of the best poets of the Great War aspired to prophetic utterance. Their brethren of the later war spoke rather of intimate hurts and misery, of uncertainties and hopelessness that the prophetic strain tended to neglect. Their mood is more puzzled, less emphatic, and their poems are often more ominous for this very reason. Rage, disgust, pity predominated in the First World War. Behind the poets of

the Second World War, beside the private grief, there is an emptiness
– the blankness of an ultimate despair:

> Father, father, I dread this air
> Blown from the far side of despair,
> The cold cold corner. What house, what hold,
> What hand is there? I look and see
> Nothing-filled eternity,
> And the great round world grows weak and old.
>
> Hold my hand, oh hold it fast –
> I am changing! – until at last
> My hand in yours no more will change,
> Though yours change on. You here, I there,
> So hand in hand, twin-leafed despair –
> I did not know death was so strange.

These quiet stanzas, from 'The Child Dying' by Edwin Muir, seem
more bleak and fearful than anything that Owen or Rosenberg wrote.
They are the poetry of annihilation, of the generations then coming
into being who face the utter devastation of the atomic bomb. Our
generations.

WORLD WAR ONE

Call to Arms:
'Men Who March Away'

THOMAS HARDY

'Men Who March Away'

(Song of the Soldiers; September 5, 1914)

What of the faith and fire within us
    Men who march away
    Ere the barn-cocks say
    Night is growing gray,
Leaving all that here can win us;
What of the faith and fire within us
    Men who march away?

Is it a purblind prank, O think you,
    Friend with the musing eye,
    Who watch us stepping by
    With doubt and dolorous sigh?
Can much pondering so hoodwink you!
Is it a purblind prank, O think you,
    Friend with the musing eye?

Nay. We well see what we are doing,
    Though some may not see –
    Dalliers as they be –
    England's need are we;
Her distress would leave us rueing:
Nay. We well see what we are doing,
    Though some may not see!

In our heart of hearts believing
    Victory crowns the just,
    And that braggarts must
    Surely bite the dust,
Press we to the field ungrieving,
In our heart of hearts believing
    Victory crowns the just.

Hence the faith and fire within us
Men who march away
Ere the barn-cocks say
Night is growing gray,
Leaving all that here can win us;
Hence the faith and fire within us
Men who march away.

ISAAC ROSENBERG

On Receiving News of the War

Snow is a strange white word.
No ice or frost
Has asked of bud or bird
For Winter's cost.

Yet ice and frost and snow
From earth to sky
This Summer land doth know.
No man knows why.

In all men's hearts it is.
Some spirit old
Hath turned with malign kiss
Our lives to mould.

Red fangs have torn His face.
God's blood is shed.
He mourns from His lone place
His children dead.

O! ancient crimson curse!
Corrode, consume.
Give back this universe
Its pristine bloom.

Cape Town, 1914

RUPERT BROOKE

The Soldier

If I should die, think only this of me:
   That there's some corner of a foreign field
That is for ever England. There shall be
   In that rich earth a richer dust concealed;
A dust whom England bore, shaped, made aware,
   Gave, once, her flowers to love, her ways to roam,
A body of England's, breathing English air,
   Washed by the rivers, blest by suns of home.

And think, this heart, all evil shed away,
   A pulse in the eternal mind, no less
      Gives somewhere back the thoughts by England
         given;
Her sights and sounds; dreams happy as her day;
   And laughter, learnt of friends; and gentleness,
      In hearts at peace, under an English heaven.

November–December 1914

EDWARD THOMAS

This is no Case of Petty Right or Wrong

This is no case of petty right or wrong
That politicians or philosophers
Can judge. I hate not Germans, nor grow hot
With love of Englishmen, to please newspapers.
Beside my hate for one fat patriot
My hatred of the Kaiser is love true: –
A kind of god he is, banging a gong.
But I have not to choose between the two,
Or between justice and injustice. Dinned
With war and argument I read no more

14

Than in the storm smoking along the wind
Athwart the wood. Two witches' cauldrons roar.
From one the weather shall rise clear and gay;
Out of the other an England beautiful
And like her mother that died yesterday.
Little I know or care if, being dull,
I shall miss something that historians
Can rake out of the ashes when perchance
The phoenix broods serene above their ken.
But with the best and meanest Englishmen
I am one in crying, God save England, lest
We lose what never slaves and cattle blessed.
The ages made her that made us from dust:
She is all we know and live by, and we trust
She is good and must endure, loving her so:
And as we love ourselves we hate our foe.

E.E. CUMMINGS

'next to of course god america i
love you land of the pilgrims and so forth oh
say can you see by the dawn's early my
country 'tis of centuries come and go
and are no more what of it we should worry
in every language even deafanddumb
thy sons acclaim your glorious name by gorry
by jingo by gee by gosh by gum
why talk of beauty what could be more beaut-
iful than these heroic happy dead
who rushed like lions to the roaring slaughter
they did not stop to think they died instead
then shall the voice of liberty be mute?'

He spoke. And drank rapidly a glass of water

EDGELL RICKWORD

The Soldier Addresses his Body

I shall be mad if you get smashed about,
we've had good times together, you and I;
although you groused a bit when luck was out,
say a girl turned us down, or we went dry.

But there's a world of things we haven't done,
countries not seen, where people do strange things;
eat fish alive, and mimic in the sun
the solemn gestures of their stone-grey kings.

I've heard of forests that are dim at noon
where snakes and creepers wrestle all day long;
where vivid beasts grow pale with the full moon,
gibber and cry, and wail a mad old song;

because at the full moon the Hippogriff
with crinkled ivory snout and agate feet,
with his green eye will glare them cold and stiff
for the coward Wyvern to come down and eat.

Vodka and kvass, and bitter mountain wines
we've never drunk, nor snatched the bursting grapes
to pelt slim girls among Sicilian vines,
who'd flicker through the leaves, faint frolic shapes.

Yes, there's a world of things we've never done,
but it's a sweat to knock them into rhyme,
let's have a drink, and give the cards a run
and leave dull verse to the dull peaceful time.

ANONYMOUS

Untitled

We mean to thrash these Prussian Pups,
We'll bag their ships, we'll smash old Krupps,
We loathe them all, the dirty swine,
We'll drown the whole lot in the Rhine.

W.B. YEATS

On Being Asked for a War Poem

I think it better that in times like these
A poet's mouth be silent, for in truth
We have no gift to set a statesman right;
He has had enough of meddling who can please
A young girl in the indolence of her youth,
Or an old man upon a winter's night.

Combat:
'Strange Hells, Strange Awaking'

ISAAC ROSENBERG

Soldier: Twentieth Century

I love you, great new Titan!
Am I not you?
Napoleon and Caesar
Out of you grew.

Out of unthinkable torture,
Eyes kissed by death,
Won back to the world again,
Lost and won in a breath,

Cruel men are made immortal,
Out of your pain born.
They have stolen the sun's power
With their feet on your shoulders worn.

Let them shrink from your girth,
That has outgrown the pallid days,
When you slept like Circe's swine,
Or a word in the brain's ways.

EDGELL RICKWORD

Winter Warfare

Colonel Cold strode up the Line
    (tabs of rime and spurs of ice);
stiffened all that met his glare:
    horses, men, and lice.

Visited a forward post,
    left them burning, ear to foot;
fingers stuck to biting steel,
    toes to frozen boot.

Stalked on into No Man's Land,
　　turned the wire to fleecy wool,
iron stakes to sugar sticks
　　snapping at a pull.

Those who watched with hoary eyes
　　saw two figures gleaming there;
Hauptmann Kälte, Colonel Cold,
　　gaunt in the grey air.

Stiffly, tinkling spurs they moved,
　　glassy-eyed, with glinting heel
stabbing those who lingered there
　　torn by screaming steel.

FREDERIC MANNING

The Trenches

Endless lanes sunken in the clay.
Bays, and traverses, fringed with wasted herbage,
Seed-pods of blue scabious, and some lingering blooms;
And the sky, seen as from a well,
Brilliant with frosty stars.
We stumble, cursing on the slippery duck-boards.
Goaded like the damned by some invisible wrath.
A will stronger than weariness, stronger than animal fear,
Implacable and monotonous.

Here a shaft, slanting, and below
A dusty and flickering light from one feeble candle
And prone figures sleeping uneasily,
Murmuring,
And men who cannot sleep,
With faces impassive as masks,
Bright, feverish eyes, and drawn lips,
Sad, pitiless, terrible faces,
Each an incarnate curse.

Here in a bay, a helmeted sentry
Silent and motionless, watching while two sleep,
And he sees before him
With indifferent eyes the blasted and torn land
Peopled with stiff prone forms, stupidly rigid,
As tho' they had not been men.

Dead are the lips where love laughed or sang,
The hands of youth eager to lay hold of life,
Eyes that have laughed to eyes,
And these were begotten,
O Love, and lived lightly, and burnt
With the lust of a man's first strength: ere they were rent,
Almost at unawares, savagely; and strewn
In bloody fragments, to be the carrion
Of rats and crows.

And the sentry moves not, searching
Night for menace with weary eyes.

WILFRED OWEN

Exposure

Our brains ache, in the merciless iced east winds that
   knive us . . .
Wearied we keep awake because the night is silent . . .
Low, drooping flares confuse our memory of the salient . . .
Worried by silence, sentries whisper, curious, nervous,
     But nothing happens.

Watching, we hear the mad gusts tugging on the wire,
Like twitching agonies of men among its brambles.
Northward, incessantly, the flickering gunnery rumbles,
Far off, like a dull rumour of some other war.
     What are we doing here?

The poignant misery of dawn begins to grow . . .
We only know war lasts, rain soaks, and clouds sag stormy.
Dawn massing in the east her melancholy army
Attacks once more in ranks on shivering ranks of gray,
     But nothing happens.

Sudden successive flights of bullets streak the silence.
Less deathly than the air that shudders black with snow,
With sidelong flowing flakes that flock, pause, and renew;
We watch them wandering up and down the wind's
   nonchalance,
     But nothing happens.

Pale flakes with fingering stealth come feeling for our
   faces –
We cringe in holes, back on forgotten dreams, and stare,
   snow-dazed,
Deep into grassier ditches. So we drowse, sun-dozed,
Littered with blossoms trickling where the blackbird fusses.
    Is it that we are dying?

Slowly our ghosts drag home: glimpsing the sunk fires,
  glozed
With crusted dark-red jewels; crickets jingle there;
For hours the innocent mice rejoice: the house is theirs;
Shutters and doors, all closed: on us the doors are closed, –
    We turn back to our dying.

Since we believe not otherwise can kind fires burn;
Nor ever suns smile true on child, or field, or fruit.
For God's invincible spring our love is made afraid;
Therefore, not loath, we lie out here; therefore were born,
    For love of God seems dying.

To-night, His frost will fasten on this mud and us,
Shrivelling many hands, puckering foreheads crisp.
The burying-party, picks and shovels in their shaking
  grasp,
Pause over half-known faces. All their eyes are ice,
    But nothing happens.

WILFRED OWEN

The Sentry

We'd found an old Boche dug-out, and he knew,
And gave us hell, for shell on frantic shell
Hammered on top, but never quite burst through.
Rain, guttering down in waterfalls of slime,
Kept slush waist-high and rising hour by hour,
And choked the steps too thick with clay to climb.
What murk of air remained stank old, and sour
With fumes of whizz-bangs, and the smell of men
Who'd lived there years, and left their curse in the den,
If not their corpses . . .
        There we herded from the blast
Of whizz-bangs, but one found our door at last, –
Buffeting eyes and breath, snuffing the candles,
And thud! flump! thud! down the steep steps came
  thumping

And sploshing in the flood, deluging muck –
The sentry's body; then, his rifle, handles
Of old Boche bombs, and mud in ruck on ruck.
We dredged him up, for killed, until he whined
'O sir, my eyes – I'm blind – I'm blind, I'm blind!'
Coaxing, I held a flame against his lids
And said if he could see the least blurred light
He was not blind; in time he'd get all right.
'I can't,' he sobbed. Eyeballs, huge-bulged like squids',
Watch my dreams still; but I forgot him there
In posting Next for duty, and sending a scout
To beg a stretcher somewhere, and flound'ring about
To other posts under the shrieking air.

*   *   *

Those other wretches, how they bled and spewed,
And one who would have drowned himself for good, –
I try not to remember these things now.
Let dread hark back for one word only: how
Half listening to that sentry's moans and jumps,
And the wild chattering of his broken teeth,
Renewed most horribly whenever crumps
Pummelled the roof and slogged the air beneath –
Through the dense din, I say, we heard him shout
'I see your lights!' But ours had long died out.

SIEGFRIED SASSOON

The Rear-Guard

(Hindenburg Line, April 1917)

Groping along the tunnel, step by step,
He winked his prying torch with patching glare
From side to side, and sniffed the unwholesome air.

Tins, boxes, bottles, shapes too vague to know;
A mirror smashed, the mattress from a bed;
And he, exploring fifty feet below
The rosy gloom of battle overhead.

Tripping, he grabbed the wall; saw someone lie
Humped at his feet, half-hidden by a rug,
And stooped to give the sleeper's arm a tug.
'I'm looking for headquarters.' No reply.
'God blast your neck!' (For days he'd had no sleep,)
'Get up and guide me through this stinking place.'

Savage, he kicked a soft, unanswering heap,
And flashed his beam across the livid face
Terribly glaring up, whose eyes yet wore
Agony dying hard ten days before;
And fists of fingers clutched a blackening wound.

Alone he staggered on until he found
Dawn's ghost that filtered down a shafted stair
To the dazed, muttering creatures underground
Who hear the boom of shells in muffled sound.
At last, with sweat of horror in his hair,
He climbed through darkness to the twilight air,
Unloading hell behind him step by step.

SIEGFRIED SASSOON

Counter-Attack

We'd gained our first objective hours before
While dawn broke like a face with blinking eyes,
Pallid, unshaved and thirsty, blind with smoke.
Things seemed all right at first. We held their line,
With bombers posted, Lewis guns well placed,
And clink of shovels deepening the shallow trench.
   The place was rotten with dead; green clumsy legs
   High-booted, sprawled and grovelled along the saps
   And trunks, face downward, in the sucking mud
   Wallowed like trodden sand-bags loosely filled;
   And naked sodden buttocks, mats of hair,
   Bulged, clotted heads slept in the plastering slime.
   And then the rain began, – the jolly old rain!

A yawning soldier knelt against the bank,
Staring across the morning blear with fog;
He wondered when the Allemands would get busy;
And then, of course, they started with five-nines
Traversing, sure as fate, and never a dud.
Mute in the clamour of shells he watched them burst
Spouting dark earth and wire with gusts from hell,
While posturing giants dissolved in drifts of smoke.
He crouched and flinched, dizzy with galloping fear,
Sick for escape, – loathing the strangled horror
And butchered, frantic gestures of the dead.

An officer came blundering down the trench:
'Stand-to and man the fire-step!' On he went . . .
Gasping and bawling, 'Fire-step . . . counter-attack!'

   Then the haze lifted. Bombing on the right
   Down the old sap: machine-guns on the left;
   And stumbling figures looming out in front.
   'O Christ, they're coming at us!' Bullets spat,
And he remembered his rifle . . . rapid fire . . .

And started blazing wildly . . . then a bang
Crumpled and spun him sideways; knocked him out
To grunt and wriggle: none heeded him; he choked
And fought the flapping veils of smothering gloom,
Lost in a blurred confusion of yells and groans . . .
Down, and down, and down, he sank and drowned,
Bleeding to death. The counter-attack had failed.

IVOR GURNEY

The Silent One

Who died on the wires, and hung there, one of two –
Who for his hours of life had chattered through
Infinite lovely chatter of Bucks accent:
Yet faced unbroken wires; stepped over, and went
A noble fool, faithful to his stripes – and ended.
But I weak, hungry, and willing only for the chance
Of line – to fight in the line, lay down under unbroken
Wires, and saw the flashes and kept unshaken,
Till the politest voice – a finicking accent, said:
'Do you think you might crawl through, there: there's
    a hole'
Darkness, shot at: I smiled, as politely replied –
'I'm afraid not, Sir.' There was no hole no way to be
    seen
Nothing but chance of death, after tearing of clothes
Kept flat, and watched the darkness, hearing bullets
    whizzing –
And thought of music – and swore deep heart's deep
    oaths
(Polite to God) and retreated and came on again,
Again retreated – and a second time faced the screen.

ROBERT SERVICE

A Pot of Tea

You make it in your mess-tin by the brazier's rosy gleam;
You watch it cloud, then settle amber clear;
You lift it with your bay'nit and you sniff the fragrant steam;
The very breath of it is ripe with cheer.
You're awful cold and dirty, and a-cursin' of your lot;
You scoff the blushin' 'alf of it, so rich and rippin' 'ot,
It bucks you up like anythink, just seems to touch the spot:
    God bless the man that first discovered Tea!

Since I came out to fight in France, which ain't the other day,
I think I've drunk enough to float a barge;
All kinds of fancy foreign dope, from caffy and doo lay,
To rum they serves you out before a charge.
In back rooms of estaminays I've gurgled pints of cham;
I've swilled down mugs of cider till I've felt a bloomin' dam;
But 'struth! they all ain't in it with the vintage of Assam:
    God bless the man that first invented Tea!

I think them lazy lumps o' gods wot kips on asphodel
Swigs nectar that's a flavour of Oolong;
I only wish them sons o'guns a-grillin' down in 'ell,
Could 'ave their daily ration of Suchong.
Hurrah! I'm off to battle, which is 'ell and 'eaven too;
And if I don't give some poor bloke a sexton's job to do,
To-night, by Fritz's camp fire, won't I 'ave a gorgeous brew
    (For fightin' mustn't interfere with Tea).
To-night we'll all be tellin' of the Boches that we slew,
    As we drink the giddy victory in Tea.

HERBERT READ

My Company

Foule! Ton âme entière est debout dans mon corps.   *Jules Romains*

I

You became
In many acts and quiet observances
A body and a soul, entire.

I cannot tell
What time your life became mine:
Perhaps when one summer night
We halted on the roadside
In the starlight only,
And you sang your sad home-songs,
Dirges which I standing outside you
Coldly condemned.

Perhaps, one night, descending cold
When rum was mighty acceptable,
And my doling gave birth to sensual gratitude.

And then our fights: we've fought together
Compact, unanimous;
And I have felt the pride of leadership.

In many acts and quiet observances
You absorbed me:
Until one day I stood eminent
And I saw you gather'd round me,
Uplooking,
And about you a radiance that seemed to beat
With variant glow and to give
Grace to our unity.

But, God! I know that I'll stand
Someday in the loneliest wilderness,

Someday my heart will cry
For the soul that has been, but that now
Is scatter'd with the winds,
Deceased and devoid.

I know that I'll wander with a cry:
'O beautiful men, O men I loved,
O whither are you gone, my company?'

2

My men go wearily
With their monstrous burdens.

They bear wooden planks
And iron sheeting
Through the area of death.

When a flare curves through the sky
They rest immobile.

Then on again,
Sweating and blaspheming –
'Oh, bloody Christ!'

My men, my modern Christs,
Your bloody agony confronts the world.

3

A man of mine
          lies on the wire.
It is death to fetch his soulless corpse.

A man of mine
          lies on the wire;
And he will rot
And first his lips
The worms will eat.
It is not thus I would have him kiss'd,
But with the warm passionate lips
Of his comrade here.

4

I can assume
A giant attitude and godlike mood,
And then detachedly regard
All riots, conflicts and collisions.

The men I've lived with
Lurch suddenly into a far perspective;
They distantly gather like a dark cloud of birds
In the autumn sky.

Urged by some unanimous
Volition or fate,
Clouds clash in opposition;
The sky quivers, the dead descend;
Earth yawns.

They are all of one species.

From my giant attitude,
In godlike mood,
I laugh till space is filled
With hellish merriment.

Then again I assume
My human docility,
Bow my head
And share their doom.

JEFFERY DAY

North Sea

Dawn on the drab North Sea! –
colourless, cold and depressing,
with the sun that we long to see
refraining from his blessing.
To the westward – sombre as doom:
to the eastward – grey and foreboding:

Comes a low, vibrating boom –
the sound of a mine exploding.

Day on the drear North Sea! –
wearisome, drab, and relentless.
The low clouds swiftly flee;
bitter the sky, and relentless.
Nothing at all in sight
save the mast of a sunken trawler,
fighting her long, last fight
with the waves that mouth and maul her.

Gale on the bleak North Sea! –
howling a dirge in the rigging.
Slowly and toilfully
through the great, grey breakers digging,
thus we make our way,
hungry, wet, and weary,
soaked with the sleet and spray,
desolate, damp and dreary.

Fog in the dank North Sea! –
silent and clammily dripping.
Slowly and mournfully,
ghostlike, goes the shipping.
Sudden across the swell
come the fog-horns hoarsely blaring
or the clang of a warning bell,
to leave us vainly staring.

Night on the black North Sea! –
black as hell's darkest hollow.
Peering anxiously,
we search for the ships that follow.
One are the sea and sky,
dim are the figures near us,
with only the sea-bird's cry
and the swish of the waves to cheer us.

Death on the wild North Sea! –
death from the shell that shatters

(death we will face with glee,
'tis the weary wait that matters): –
death from the guns that roar,
and the splinters weirdly shrieking.
'Tis a fight to the death; 'tis war,
and the North Sea is redly reeking!

RUDYARD KIPLING

A Drifter Off Tarentum

He from the wind-bitten North with ship and companions descended,
Searching for eggs of death spawned by invisible hulls.
Many he found and drew forth. Of a sudden the fishery ended
In flame and a clamorous breath known to the eye-pecking gulls.

ISAAC ROSENBERG

The Troop Ship

Grotesque and queerly huddled
Contortionists to twist
The sleepy soul to a sleep,
We lie all sorts of ways
And cannot sleep.
The wet wind is so cold,
And the lurching men so careless,
That, should you drop to a doze,
Winds' fumble or men's feet
Are on your face.

ANONYMOUS

The Pilot's Psalm

The BE2c is my 'bus; therefore I shall want.
He maketh me to come down in green pastures.
He leadeth me where I will not go.
He maketh me to be sick; he leadeth me astray on all
    cross-country flights.
Yea, though I fly over No-man's land where mine
    enemies would compass me about, I fear much evil
    for thou art with me; thy joystick and thy prop discomfort me.
Thou preparest a crash before me in the presence
    of thy enemies; thy RAF anointeth my hair with oil,
    thy tank leaketh badly.
Surely to goodness thou shalt not follow me all
    the days of my life; else I shall dwell in the House of
    Colney Hatch forever.

RUDYARD KIPLING

R.A.F. (Aged Eighteen)

Laughing through clouds, his milk-teeth still unshed,
Cities and men he smote from overhead.
His deaths delivered, he returned to play
Childlike, with childish things not put away.

WORLD WAR ONE

'Come, Death . . .'

WALTER DE LA MARE

Motley

Come, Death, I'd have a word with thee;
And thou, poor Innocency;
And Love – a lad with broken wing;
And Pity, too:
The Fool shall sing to you,
As Fools will sing.

Ay, music hath small sense,
And a tune's soon told,
And Earth is old,
And my poor wits are dense;
Yet have I secrets, – dark, my dear,
To breathe you all. Come near.
And lest some hideous listener tells,
I'll ring my bells.

They are all at war! –
Yes, yes, their bodies go
'Neath burning sun and icy star
To chaunted songs of woe,
Dragging cold cannon through a mire
Of rain and blood and spouting fire,
The new moon glinting hard on eyes
Wide with insanities!

Hush! . . . I use words
I hardly know the meaning of;
And the mute birds
Are glancing at Love
From out their shade of leaf and flower,
Trembling at treacheries
Which even in noonday cower.
Heed, heed not what I said
Of frenzied hosts of men,
More fools than I,

On envy, hatred fed,
Who kill, and die –
Spake I not plainly, then?
Yet Pity whispered, 'Why?'

Thou silly thing, off to thy daisies go.
Mine was not news for child to know,
And Death – no ears hath. He hath supped where creep
Eyeless worms in hush of sleep;
Yet, when he smiles, the hand he draws
Athwart his grinning jaws –
Faintly the thin bones rattle, and – there, there!
Hearken how my bells in the air
Drive away care! . . .

Nay, but a dream I had
Of a world all mad.
Not simple happy mad like me,
Who am mad like an empty scene
Of water and willow tree,
Where the wind hath been;
But that foul Satan-mad,
Who rots in his own head,
And counts the dead,
Not honest one – and two –
But for the ghosts they were,
Brave, faithful, true,
When, head in air,
In Earth's clear green and blue
Heaven they did share
With beauty who bade them there. . . .

There, now! Death goes –
Mayhap I've wearied him.
Ay, and the light doth dim,
And asleep's the rose,
And tired Innocence
In dreams is hence. . . .
Come, Love, my lad,
Nodding that drowsy head,
'Tis time thy prayers were said!

JOHN McRAE

In Flanders Fields

In Flanders fields the poppies blow
Between the crosses, row on row
   That mark our place; and in the sky
   The larks, still bravely singing, fly
Scarce heard amid the guns below.

We are the Dead. Short days ago
We lived, felt dawn, saw sunset glow,
   Loved and were loved, and now we lie
      In Flanders fields.

Take up our quarrel with the foe:
To you from failing hands we throw
   The torch; be yours to hold it high.
   If ye break faith with us who die
We shall not sleep, though poppies grow
      In Flanders fields.

MAX PLOWMAN

The Dead Soldiers

1

Spectrum Trench. Autumn. Nineteen-Sixteen.
And Zenith. (The Border Regiment will remember.)
A little north of where Lesboeufs had been.
(The Australians took it over in December.)
Just as the scythe had caught them, there they lay,
A sheaf for Death, ungarnered and untied:
A crescent moon of men who showed the way
When first the Tanks crept out, till they too died:
Guardsmen, I think, but one could hardly tell,
It was a forward slope, beyond the crest,
Muddier than any place in Dante's hell,
Where sniping gave us very little rest.
At night one stumbled over them and swore;
Each day the rain hid them a little more.

2

Fantastic forms, in posturing attitudes,
Twisted and bent, or lying deathly prone;
Their individual hopes my thought eludes,
But each man had a hope to call his own.
Much else? – God knows. But not for me the thought,
'Your mothers made your bodies: God your souls,
And, for because you dutifully fought,
God will go mad and make of half-lives, wholes.'
No. God in every one of you was slain;
For killing men is always killing God,
Though life destroyed shall come to life again
And loveliness rise from the sodden sod.
But if of life we do destroy the best,
God wanders wide, and weeps in his unrest.

1917

W.B. YEATS

An Irish Airman Foresees His Death

I know that I shall meet my fate
Somewhere among the clouds above;
Those that I fight I do not hate,
Those that I guard I do not love;
My country is Kiltartan Cross,
My countrymen Kiltartan's poor,
No likely end could bring them loss
Or leave them happier than before.
Nor law, nor duty bade me fight,
Nor public men, nor cheering crowds,
A lonely impulse of delight
Drove to this tumult in the clouds;
I balanced all, brought all to mind,
The years to come seemed waste of breath,
A waste of breath the years behind
In balance with this life, this death.

ISAAC ROSENBERG

Dead Man's Dump

The plunging limbers over the shattered track
Racketed with their rusty freight,
Stuck out like many crowns of thorns,
And the rusty stakes like sceptres old
To stay the flood of brutish men
Upon our brothers dear.

The wheels lurched over sprawled dead
But pained them not, though their bones
   crunched,
Their shut mouths made no moan.

They lie there huddled, friend and foeman,
Man born of man, and born of woman,
And shells go crying over them
From night till night and now.

Earth has waited for them,
All the time of their growth
Fretting for their decay:
Now she has them at last!
In the strength of their strength
Suspended – stopped and held.

What fierce imaginings their dark souls lit?
Earth! have they gone into you!
Somewhere they must have gone,
And flung on your hard back
Is their soul's sack
Emptied of God-ancestralled essences.
Who hurled them out? Who hurled?

None saw their spirits' shadow shake the grass,
Or stood aside for the half used life to pass
Out of those doomed nostrils and the
    doomed mouth,
When the swift iron burning bee
Drained the wild honey of their youth.

What of us who, flung on the shrieking pyre,
Walk, our usual thoughts untouched,
Our lucky limbs as on ichor fed,
Immortal seeming ever?
Perhaps when the flames beat loud on us,
A fear may choke in our veins
And the startled blood may stop.

The air is loud with death,
The dark air spurts with fire,
The explosions ceaseless are.
Timelessly now, some minutes past,
These dead strode time with vigorous life,
Till the shrapnel called 'An end!'

But not to all. In bleeding pangs
Some borne on stretchers dreamed of home,
Dear things, war-blotted from their hearts.

Maniac Earth! howling and flying, your bowel
Seared by the jagged fire, the iron love,
The impetuous storm of savage love.
Dark Earth! dark Heavens! swinging in
   chemic smoke,
What dead are born when you kiss each
   soundless soul
With lightning and thunder from your
   mined heart,
Which man's self dug, and his blind fingers loosed?

A man's brains splattered on
A stretcher-bearer's face;
His shook shoulders slipped their load,
But when they bent to look again
The drowning soul was sunk too deep
For human tenderness.

They left this dead with the older dead,
Stretched at the cross roads.

Burnt black by strange decay
Their sinister faces lie,
The lid over each eye,
The grass and coloured clay
More motion have than they,
Joined to the great sunk silences.

Here is one not long dead;
His dark hearing caught our far wheels,
And the choked soul stretched weak hands
To reach the living word the far wheels said,
The blood-dazed intelligence beating for light,
Crying through the suspense of the far torturing wheels
Swift for the end to break
Or the wheels to break,
Cried as the tide of the world broke over his sight.

Will they come? Will they ever come?
Even as the mixed hoofs of the mules,
The quivering-bellied mules,
And the rushing wheels all mixed
With his tortured upturned sight.
So we crashed round the bend,
We heard his weak scream,
We heard his very last sound,
And our wheels grazed his dead face.

RUDYARD KIPLING

Unknown Female Corpse

Headless, lacking foot and hand,
Horrible I come to land.
I beseech all women's sons
Know I was a mother once.

RUDYARD KIPLING

A Death-bed

'This is the State above the Law.
   The State exists for the State alone.'
(*This is a gland at the back of the jaw,*
   And an answering lump by the collar-bone.)

Some die shouting in gas or fire;
   Some die silent, by shell and shot.
Some die desperate, caught on the wire;
   Some die suddenly. This will not.

'Regis suprema voluntas Lex'
   (*It will follow the regular course of – throats.*)
Some die pinned by the broken decks,
   Some die sobbing between the boats.

Some die eloquent, pressed to death
   By the sliding trench, as their friends can hear.
Some die wholly in half a breath.
   Some – give trouble for half a year.

'There is neither Evil nor Good in life
   Except as the needs of the State ordain.'
(*Since it is rather too late for the knife,*
   All we can do is to mask the pain.)

Some die saintly in faith and hope –
   One died thus in a prison yard –
Some die broken by rape or the rope;
   Some die easily. This dies hard.

'I will dash to pieces who bar my way.
   Woe to the traitor! Woe to the weak!'
(*Let him write what he wishes to say.*
   It tires him out if he tries to speak.)

Some die quietly. Some abound
   In loud self-pity. Others spread
Bad morale through the cots around . . .
   This is a type that is better dead.

'The war was forced on me by my foes.
   All that I sought was the right to live.'
(*Don't be afraid of a triple dose;*
   The pain will neutralize half we give.

Here are the needles. See that he dies
   While the effects of the drug endure . . .
What is the question he asks with his eyes? –
   Yes, All-Highest, to God, be sure.)

PATRICK MACGILL

Matey

(Cambrin, May 1915)

Not comin' back tonight, matey,
And reliefs are coming through.
We're all goin' out all right, matey,
Only we're leaving you.
Gawd! it's a bloody sin, matey,
Now that we've finished the fight.
We go when reliefs come in, matey,
But you're stayin' 'ere tonight.

Over the top is cold, matey –
You lie on the field alone.
Didn't I love you of old, matey,
Dearer than the blood of my own?
You were my dearest chum, matey –
(Gawd! but your face is white)
But now, though reliefs 'ave come, matey,
I'm goin' alone tonight.

I'd sooner the bullet was mine, matey –
Goin' out on my own.
Leavin' you 'ere in the line, matey,
All by yourself, alone,
Chum o' mine and you're dead, matey,
And this is the way we part,
The bullet went through your head, matey,
But Gawd! it went through my 'eart.

WILFRED OWEN

Conscious

His fingers wake, and flutter; up the bed.
His eyes come open with a pull of will,
Helped by the yellow may-flowers by his head.
The blind-cord drawls across the window-sill . . .
What a smooth floor the ward has! What a rug!
Who is that talking somewhere out of sight?
Why are they laughing? What's inside that jug?
'Nurse! Doctor!' – 'Yes; all right, all right.'

But sudden evening muddles all the air –
There seems no time to want a drink of water,
Nurse looks so far away. And here and there
Music and roses burst through crimson slaughter.
He can't remember where he saw blue sky.
More blankets. Cold. He's cold. And yet so hot.
And there's no light to see the voices by;
There is no time to ask – he knows not what.

EDGELL RICKWORD

Moonrise Over Battlefield

After the fallen sun the wind was sad
like violins behind immense old walls.
Trees were musicians swaying round the bed
Of a woman in gloomy halls.

In privacy of music she made ready
with comb and silver dust and fard;
under his silken vest her little belly
shone like a bladder of sweet lard.

She drifted with the grand air of a punk
on Heaven's streets soliciting white saints;
then lay in bright communion on a cloud-bank
as one who near extreme of pleasure faints.

Then I thought, standing in the ruined trench,
(all round, dead Boche white-shirted lay like sheep),
'Why does this damned entrancing bitch
seek lovers only among them that sleep?'

ISAAC ROSENBERG

Returning, *We hear the Larks*

Sombre the night is.
And though we have our lives, we know
What sinister threat lurks there.

Dragging these anguished limbs, we only know
This poison-blasted track opens on our camp –
On a little safe sleep.

But hark! joy – joy – strange joy.

Lo! heights of night ringing with unseen larks.
Music showering on our upturned list'ning faces.

Death could drop from the dark
As easily as song –
But song only dropped,
Like a blind man's dreams on the sand
By dangerous tides,
Like a girl's dark hair for she dreams no
   ruin lies there,
Or her kisses where a serpent hides.

EDWARD THOMAS

Lights Out

I have come to the borders of sleep,
The unfathomable deep
Forest where all must lose
Their way, however straight,
Or winding, soon or late;
They cannot choose.

Many a road and track
That, since the dawn's first crack,
Up to the forest brink,
Deceived the travellers,
Suddenly now blurs,
And in they sink.

Here love ends,
Despair, ambition ends,
All pleasure and all trouble,
Although most sweet or bitter,
Here ends in sleep that is sweeter
Than tasks most noble.

There is not any book
Or face of dearest look
That I would not turn from now
To go into the unknown
I must enter and leave alone
I know not how.

The tall forest towers;
Its cloudy foliage lowers
Ahead, shelf above shelf;
Its silence I hear and obey
That I may lose my way
And myself.

EDWARD THOMAS

Rain

Rain, midnight rain, nothing but the wild rain
On this bleak hut, and solitude, and me
Remembering again that I shall die
And neither hear the rain nor give it thanks
For washing me cleaner than I have been
Since I was born into this solitude.
Blessed are the dead that the rain rains upon:
But here I pray that none whom once I loved
Is dying to-night or lying still awake
Solitary, listening to the rain,
Either in pain or thus in sympathy
Helpless among the living and the dead,
Like a cold water among broken reeds,
Myriads of broken reeds all still and stiff,
Like me who have no love which this wild rain
Has not dissolved except the love of death,
If love it be for what is perfect and
Cannot, the tempest tells me, disappoint.

CHARLES HAMILTON SORLEY

Sonnet

When you see millions of the mouthless dead
Across your dreams in pale battalions go,
Say not soft things, as other men have said,
That you'll remember. For you need not so.
Give them not praise. For, deaf, how should they know
It is not curses heaped on each gashed head?
Nor tears. Their blind eyes see not your tears flow.
Nor honour. It is easy to be dead.
Say only this, 'They are dead'. Then add thereto,
'Yet many a better one has died before'.
Then, scanning all the o'ercrowded mass, should you
Perceive one face that you loved heretofore,
It is a spook. None wears the face you knew.
Great death has made all his for evermore.

Disgust:

'The Old Lie – Dulce et decorum
est pro patria mori'

CHARLES HAMILTON SORLEY

Untitled

All the hills and vales along
Earth is bursting into song,
And the singers are the chaps
Who are going to die perhaps.
　O sing, marching men,
　Till the valleys ring again.
　Give your gladness to earth's keeping,
　So be glad, when you are sleeping.

Cast away regret and rue,
Think what you are marching to,
Little live, great pass.
Jesus Christ and Barabbas
Were found the same day.
This died, that, went his way.
　So sing with joyful breath.
　For why, you are going to death.
　Teeming earth will surely store
　All the gladness that you pour.

Earth that never doubts nor fears
Earth that knows of death, not tears,
Earth that bore with joyful ease
Hemlock for Socrates,
Earth that blossomed and was glad
'Neath the cross that Christ had,
Shall rejoice and blossom too
When the bullet reaches you.
　Wherefore, men marching
　On the road to death, sing!
　Pour gladness on earth's head,
　So be merry, so be dead.

From the hills and valleys earth
Shouts back the sound of mirth,
Tramp of feet and lilt of song
Ringing all the road along.
All the music of their going,
Ringing swinging glad song-throwing,
Earth will echo still, when foot
Lies numb and voice mute.
 On marching men, on
 To the gates of death with song.
 Sow your gladness for earth's reaping,
 So you may be glad though sleeping.
 Strew your gladness on earth's bed,
 So be merry, so be dead.

E.E. CUMMINGS

i sing of Olaf glad and big
whose warmest heart recoiled at war;
a conscientious object-or

his wellbelovéd colonel(trig
westpointer most succinctly bred)
took erring Olaf soon in hand;
but – though an host of overjoyed
noncoms(first knocking on the head
him)do through icy waters roll
that helplessness which others stroke
with brushes recently employed
anent this muddy toiletbowl,
while kindred intellects evoke
allegiance per blunt instruments –
Olaf(being to all intents
a corpse and wanting any rag
upon what God unto him gave)
responds, without getting annoyed
'I will not kiss your f.ing flag'

straightway the silver bird looked grave
(departing hurriedly to shave)

but – though all kinds of officers
(a yearning nation's blueeyed pride)
their passive prey did kick and curse
until for wear their clarion
voices and boots were much the worse,
and egged the firstclassprivates on
his rectum wickedly to tease
by means of skilfully applied
bayonets roasted hot with heat –
Olaf(upon what were once knees)
does almost ceaselessly repeat
'there is some s. I will not eat'

our president, being of which
assertions duly notified
threw the yellowsonofabitch
into a dungeon, where he died

Christ(of His mercy infinite)
i pray to see;and Olaf, too

preponderatingly because
unless statistics lie he was
more brave than me:more blond than you.

SIEGFRIED SASSOON

Suicide in the Trenches

I knew a simple soldier boy
Who grinned at life in empty joy,
Slept soundly through the lonesome dark,
And whistled early with the lark.

In winter trenches, cowed and glum,
With crumps and lice and lack of rum,
He put a bullet through his brain.
No one spoke of him again.

You smug-faced crowds with kindling eye
Who cheer when soldier lads march by,
Sneak home and pray you'll never know
The hell where youth and laughter go.

A.P. HERBERT

Untitled*

The General inspecting the trenches
Exclaimed with a horrified shout,
'I refuse to command a Division
Which leaves its excreta about.'

But nobody took any notice
No one was prepared to refute,
That the presence of shit was congenial
Compared with the presence of Shute.

And certain responsible critics
Made haste to reply to his words
Observing that his Staff advisers
Consisted entirely of turds.

For shit may be shot at odd corners
And paper supplied there to suit.
But a shit would be shot without mourners
If somebody shot that shit Shute.

---

* This poem is attributed to A.P. Herbert in Lyn Macdonald's *Somme*. Herbert served with the Royal Naval Division 1914–17 in Gallipoli and in France, where he was wounded. Major-General C.D. (later Lieutenant-General Sir Cameron, KCB, KCMG) Shute complained about the state of trenches which the Naval Division had just taken over from Portuguese units – this poem was the troops' reply. Shute was honoured after the war, and in 1927 was GOC-in-C, Northern Command, having been Lieutenant of the Tower of London 1926–7. Died 1936.

H. SMALLEY SARSON

The Shell

Shrieking its message the flying death
Cursed the resisting air,
Then buried its nose by a battered church,
A skeleton gaunt and bare.

The brains of science, the money of fools
Had fashioned an iron slave
Destined to kill, yet the futile end
Was a child's uprooted grave.

ANONYMOUS

I Don't Want to be a Soldier

I don't want to be a soldier,
I don't want to go to war.
I'd rather stay at home,
Around the streets to roam,
And live on the earnings of a well-paid whore.
I don't want a bayonet up my arse-hole,
I don't want my ballocks shot away.
I'd rather stay in England,
In merry merry England,
And fuck my bloody life away.

WILFRED OWEN

Dulce et decorum est

Bent double, like old beggars under sacks,
Knock-kneed, coughing like hags, we cursed through
    sludge,
Till on the haunting flares we turned our backs
And towards our distant rest began to trudge.
Men marched asleep. Many had lost their boots
But limped on, blood-shod. All went lame; all blind;

Drunk with fatigue; deaf even to the hoots
Of gas shells dropping softly behind.

Gas! GAS! Quick, boys! – An ecstasy of fumbling,
Fitting the clumsy helmets just in time;
But someone still was yelling out and stumbling,
And flound'ring like a man in fire or lime . . .
Dim, through the misty panes and thick green light,
As under a green sea, I saw him drowning.

In all my dreams, before my helpless sight,
He plunges at me, guttering, choking, drowning.

If in some smothering dreams you too could pace
Behind the wagon that we flung him in,
And watch the white eyes writhing in his face,
His hanging face, like a devil's sick of sin;
If you could hear, at every jolt, the blood
Come gargling from the froth-corrupted lungs,
Obscene as cancer, bitter as the cud
Of vile, incurable sores on innocent tongues, –
My friend, you would not tell with such high zest
To children ardent for some desperate glory,
The old Lie: Dulce et decorum est
Pro patria mori.

ROBERT GRAVES

Dead Cow Farm

An ancient saga tells us how
In the beginning the First Cow
(For nothing living yet had birth
But elemental cow on earth)
Began to lick cold stones and mud:
Under her warm tongue flesh and blood
Blossomed, a miracle to believe;
And so was Adam born, and Eve.
Here now is chaos once again,
Primaeval mud, cold stones and rain,
Here flesh decays and blood drips red,
And the Cow's dead, the old Cow's dead.

CHARLES HAMILTON SORLEY

A Hundred Thousand Million Mites

A hundred thousand million mites we go
Wheeling and tacking o'er the endless plain,
Some black with death – and some are white with woe.
Who sent us forth? Who takes us home again?

And there is sound of hymns of praise – to whom?
And curses – on whom curses? – snap the air.
And there is hope goes hand in hand with gloom,
And blood and indignation and despair.

And there is murmuring of the multitude
And blindness, and great blindness, until some
Step forth and challenge blind Vicissitude
Who tramples on them: so that fewer come.

And nations, ankle-deep in love or hate,
Throw darts or kisses all the unwitting hour
Beside the ominous unseen tide of fate;
And there is emptiness and drink and power.

And some are mounted on swift steeds of thought
And some drag sluggish feet of stable toil.
Yet all, as though they furiously sought,
Twist turn and tussle, close and cling and coil.

A hundred thousand million mites we sway
Writhing and tossing on the eternal plain,
Some black with death – but most are bright with Day!
Who sent us forth? Who brings us home again?

WILFRED OWEN

A Terre

(Being the Philosophy of Many Soldiers)

Sit on the bed. I'm blind, and three parts shell.
Be careful; can't shake hands now; never shall.
Both arms have mutinied against me, – brutes.
My fingers fidget like ten idle brats.

I tried to peg out soldierly, – no use!
One dies of war like any old disease.
This bandage feels like pennies on my eyes.
I have my medals? – Discs to make eyes close.
My glorious ribbons? – Ripped from my own back
In scarlet shreds. (That's for your poetry book.)

A short life and a merry one, my buck!
We used to say we'd hate to live dead-old, –
Yet now . . . I'd willingly be puffy, bald,
And patriotic. Buffers catch from boys
At least the jokes hurled at them. I suppose
Little I'd ever teach a son, but hitting,
Shooting, war, hunting, all the arts of hurting.
Well, that's what I learnt, – that, and making money.

Your fifty years ahead seem none to many?
Tell me how long I've got? God! For one year
To help myself to nothing more than air!
One Spring! Is one too good to spare, too long?
Spring wind would work its own way to my lung,
And grow me legs as quick as lilac-shoots.

My servant's lamed, but listen how he shouts!
When I'm lugged out, he'll still be good for that.
Here in this mummy-case, you know, I've thought
How well I might have swept his floors for ever.
I'd ask no nights off when the bustle's over,

Enjoying so the dirt. Who's prejudiced
Against a grimed hand when his own's quite dust,
Less live than specks that in the sun-shafts turn,
Less warm than dust that mixes with arms' tan?
I'd love to be a sweep, now, black as Town,
Yes, or a muckman. Must I be his load?

O Life, Life, let me breathe, – a dug-out rat!
Not worse than ours the existences rats lead –
Nosing along at night down some safe rut,
They find a shell-proof home before they rot.
Dead men may envy living mites in cheese,
Or good germs even. Microbes have their joys,
And subdivide, and never come to death.
Certainly flowers have the easiest time on earth.
'I shall be one with nature, herb, and stone',
Shelley would tell me. Shelley would be stunned:

The dullest Tommy hugs that fancy now.
'Pushing up daisies' is their creed, you know.
To grain, then, go my fat, to buds my sap,
For all the usefulness there is in soap.
D'you think the Boche will ever stew man-soup?
Some day, no doubt, if . . .
                              Friend, be very sure
I shall be better off with plants that share
More peaceably the meadow and the shower.
Soft rains will touch me, – as they could touch once,
And nothing but the sun shall make me ware.
Your guns may crash around me. I'll not hear;
Or, if I wince, I shall not know I wince.
Don't take my soul's poor comfort for your jest.
Soldiers may grow a soul when turned to fronds,
But here the thing's best left at home with friends.

My soul's a little grief, grappling your chest,
To climb your throat on sobs; easily chased
On other sighs and wiped by fresher winds.

Carry my crying spirit till it's weaned
To do without what blood remained these wounds.

WILFRED OWEN

Insensibility

I

Happy are men who yet before they are killed
Can let their veins run cold.
Whom no compassion fleers
Or makes their feet
Sore on the alleys cobbled with their brothers.
The front line withers,
But they are troops who fade, not flowers
For poets' tearful fooling:
Men, gaps for filling:
Losses, who might have fought
Longer; but no one bothers.

2

And some cease feeling
Even themselves or for themselves.
Dullness best solves
The tease and doubt of shelling,
And Chance's strange arithmetic
Comes simpler than the reckoning of their shilling.
They keep no check on armies' decimation.

3

Happy are these who lose imagination:
They have enough to carry with ammunition.
Their spirit drags no pack,
Their old wounds, save with cold, can not more ache,
Having seen all things red,
Their eyes are rid
Of the hurt of the colour of blood for ever.
And terror's first constriction over,
Their hearts remain small-drawn.
Their senses in some scorching cautery of battle
Now long since ironed,
Can laugh among the dying, unconcerned.

4

Happy the soldier home, with not a notion
How somewhere, every dawn, some men attack,
And many sighs are drained.
Happy the lad whose mind was never trained:
His days are worth forgetting more than not.
He sings along the march
Which we march taciturn, because of dusk,
The long, forlorn, relentless trend
From larger day to huger night.

5

We wise, who with a thought besmirch
Blood over all our soul,
How should we see our task
But through his blunt and lashless eyes?
Alive, he is not vital overmuch;
Dying, not mortal overmuch;
Nor sad, nor proud,
Nor curious at all.
He cannot tell
Old men's placidity from his.

6

But cursed are dullards whom no cannon stuns,
That they should be as stones;
Wretched are they, and mean
With paucity that never was simplicity.
By choice they made themselves immune
To pity and whatever mourns in man
Before the last sea and the hapless stars;
Whatever mourns when many leave these shores;
Whatever shares
The eternal reciprocity of tears.

JOHN PEALE BISHOP

In the Dordogne

We stood up before day
and shaved by metal mirrors
in the faint flame of a faulty candle.

And we hurried down the wide stone stairs
with a clirr of spurr chains
on stone. And we thought
when the cocks crew
that the ghosts of a dead dawn
would rise and be off. But they stayed
under the window, crouched on the staircase,
the window now the colour of morning.

The colonel slept in the bed of Sully,
slept on: but we descended
and saw in a niche in the white wall
a Virgin and child, serene
who were stone: we saw sycamore:
three aged mages
scattering gifts of gold.
But when the wind blew, there were autumn odours
and the shadowed trees
had the dapplings of young fawns.

And each day one died or another
died: each week we sent out thousands
that returned by hundreds
wounded or gassed. And those that died
we buried close to the old wall
within a stone's throw of Perigord
under the tower of the troubadours.

And because we had courage;
because there was courage and youth
ready to be wasted; because we endured

and were prepared for all the endurance;
we thought something must come of it:
that the Virgin would raise her child and smile;
the trees gather up their gold and go;
that courage would avail something
and something we had never lost
be regained through wastage, by dying,
by burying the others under the English tower.

The colonel slept on in the bed of Sully
under the ravelling curtains: the leaves fell
and were blown away: the young men rotted
under the shadow of the tower
in a land of small clear silent streams
where the coming on of evening is
the letting down of blue and azure veils
over the clear and silent streams
delicately bordered by poplars.

ISAAC ROSENBERG

Break of Day in the Trenches

The darkness crumbles away –
It is the same old druid Time as ever.
Only a live thing leaps my hand –
A queer sardonic rat –
As I pull the parapet's poppy
To stick behind my ear.
Droll rat, they would shoot you if they knew
Your cosmopolitan sympathies.
Now you have touched this English hand
You will do the same to a German –
Soon, no doubt, if it be your pleasure
To cross the sleeping green between.
It seems you inwardly grin as you pass
Strong eyes, fine limbs, haughty athletes
Less chanced than you for life,
Bonds to the whims of murder,
Sprawled in the bowels of the earth,
The torn fields of France.
What do you see in our eyes
At the shrieking iron and flame
Hurled through still heavens?
What quaver – what heart aghast?
Poppies whose roots are in man's veins
Drop, and are ever dropping;
But mine in my ear is safe,
Just a little white with the dust.

SIEGFRIED SASSOON

Does it Matter

Does it matter? – losing your legs? . . .
For people will always be kind,
And you need not show that you mind
When the others come in after hunting
To gobble their muffins and eggs.

Does it matter? – losing your sight? . . .
There's such splendid work for the blind;
And people will always be kind,
As you sit on the terrace remembering
And turning your face to the light.

Do they matter? – those dreams from the pit? . . .
You can drink and forget and be glad,
And people won't say that you're mad;
For they'll know you've fought for your country
And no one will worry a bit.

OSBERT SITWELL

from How Shall we Rise to Greet the Dawn?

Continually they cackle thus,
These venerable birds,
Crying, 'Those whom the Gods love
Die young'
Or something of that sort.

Home Front:
'The Singing Birds are Mute'

WILFRED OWEN

The Send-Off

Down the close darkening lanes they sang their way
To the siding-shed,
And lined the train with faces grimly gay.

Their breasts were stuck all white with wreath and spray
As men's are, dead.

Dull porters watched them, and a casual tramp
Stood staring hard,
Sorry to miss them from the upland camp.
Then, unmoved, signals nodded, and a lamp
Winked to the guard.

So secretly, like wrongs hushed-up, they went.
They were not ours:
We never heard to which front these were sent.

Nor there if they yet mock what women meant
Who gave them flowers.

Shall they return to beatings of great bells
In wild train-loads?
A few, a few, too few for drums and yells,

May creep back, silent, to village wells,
Up half-known roads.

SIEGFRIED SASSOON

'Blighters'

The House is crammed: tier beyond tier they grin
And cackle at the Show, while prancing ranks
Of harlots shrill the chorus, drunk with din;
'We're sure the Kaiser loves our dear old Tanks!'

I'd like to see a Tank come down the stalls,
Lurching to rag-time tunes, or 'Home, sweet Home',
And there'd be no more jokes in Music-halls
To mock the riddled corpses round Bapaume.

SIEGFRIED SASSOON

Memorial Tablet

(Great War, 1918)

Squire nagged and bullied till I went to fight
(Under Lord Derby's scheme). I died in hell –
(They called it Passchendaele); my wound was slight,
And I was hobbling back, and then a shell
Burst slick upon the duck-boards; so I fell
Into the bottomless mud, and lost the light.

In sermon-time, while Squire is in his pew,
He gives my gilded name a thoughtful stare;
For though low down upon the list, I'm there:
'In proud and glorious memory' – that's my due.
Two bleeding years I fought in France for Squire;
I suffered anguish that he's never guessed;
Once I came home on leave; and then went west.
What greater glory could a man desire?

EWART ALAN MACKINTOSH

In Memoriam

Private D. Sutherland killed in action
in the German trench, May 16th, 1916,
and the others who died

So you were David's father,
And he was your only son,
And the new-cut peats are rotting
And the work is left undone,
Because of an old man weeping,
Just an old man in pain,
For David, his son David,
That will not come again.

Oh, the letters he wrote you
And I can see them still,
Not a word of the fighting
But just the sheep on the hill
And how you should get the crops in
Ere the year got stormier,
And the Bosches have got his body,
And I was his officer.

You were only David's father,
But I had fifty sons
When we went up in the evening
Under the arch of the guns,
And we came back at twilight –
O God! I heard them call
To me for help and pity
That could not help at all.

Oh, never will I forget you,
My men that trusted me,
More my sons than your fathers',
For they could only see
The little helpless babies

And the young men in their pride.
They could not see you dying,
And hold you while you died.

Happy and young and gallant,
They saw their first-born go,
But not the strong limbs broken
And the beautiful men brought low,
The piteous writhing bodies,
They screamed 'Don't leave me, sir,'
For they were only your fathers
But I was your officer.

ANONYMOUS

I've lost my rifle and bayonet,
I've lost my pull-through too,
I've lost the socks that you sent me
That lasted the whole winter through,
I've lost the razor that shaved me,
I've lost my four-by-two,
I've lost my hold-all and now I've got damn all
Since I've lost you.

RUDYARD KIPLING

A Dead Statesman

I could not dig; I dared not rob;
Therefore I lied to please the mob.
Now all my lies are proved untrue
And I must face the men I slew.
What tale shall serve me here among
Mine angry and defrauded young?

D.H. LAWRENCE

Tommies in the Train

The sun shines,
The coltsfoot flowers along the railway banks
Shine like flat coin which Jove in thanks
Strews each side the lines.

A steeple
In purple elms, daffodils
Sparkle beneath; luminous hills
Beyond – and no people.

England, O Danaë
To this spring of cosmic gold
That falls on your lap of mould! –
What then are we?

What are we
Clay-coloured, who roll in fatigue
As the train falls league after league
From our destiny?

A hand is over my face,
A cold hand. – I peep between the fingers
To watch the world that lingers
Behind, yet keeps pace.

Always there, as I peep
Between the fingers that cover my face!
Which then is it that falls from its place
And rolls down the steep?

Is it the train
That falls like a meteorite
Backward into space, to alight
Never again?

Or is it the illusory world
That falls from reality
As we look? Or are we
Like a thunderbolt hurled?

One or another
Is lost, since we fall apart
Endlessly, in one motion depart
From each other.

IVOR GURNEY

To His Love

He's gone, and all our plans
    Are useless indeed.
We'll walk no more on Cotswold
    Where the sheep feed
    Quietly and take no heed.

His body that was so quick
    Is not as you
Knew it, on Severn river
    Under the blue
    Driving our small boat through.

You would not know him now . . .
    But still he died
Nobly, so cover him over
    With violets of pride
    Purple from Severn side.

Cover him, cover him soon!
    And with thick-set
Masses of memoried flowers –
    Hide that red wet
    Thing I must somehow forget.

ISAAC ROSENBERG

'A Worm fed on the heart of Corinth'

A worm fed on the heart of Corinth,
Babylon and Rome:
Not Paris raped tall Helen,
But this incestuous worm,
Who lured her vivid beauty
To his amorphous sleep.
England! famous as Helen
Is thy betrothal sung
To him the shadowless,
More amorous than Solomon.

EDWARD THOMAS

Fifty Faggots

There they stand, on their ends, the fifty faggots
That once were underwood of hazel and ash
In Jenny Pinks's Copse. Now, by the hedge
Close packed, they make a thicket fancy alone
Can creep through with the mouse and wren.
   Next spring
A blackbird or a robin will nest there,
Accustomed to them, thinking they will remain
Whatever is for ever to a bird:
This Spring it is too late; the swift has come.
'Twas a hot day for carrying them up:
Better they will never warm me, though they must
Light several Winters' fires. Before they are done
The war will have ended, many other things
Have ended, maybe, that I can no more
Foresee or more control than robin and wren.

THOMAS HARDY

In Time of 'The Breaking of Nations'

Only a man harrowing clods
In a slow silent walk
With an old horse that stumbles and nods
Half asleep as they stalk.

Only thin smoke without flame
From the heaps of couch-grass:
Yet this will go onward the same
Though Dynasties pass.

Yonder a maid and her wight
Come whispering by:
War's annals will fade into night
Ere their story die.

1915

WORLD WAR ONE

Aftermath:
'Let Us Sleep Now . . .'

WILFRED OWEN

Strange Meeting

It seemed that out of battle I escaped
Down some profound dull tunnel, long since scooped
Through granites which titanic wars had groined.
Yet also there encumbered sleepers groaned,
Too fast in thought or death to be bestirred.
Then, as I probed them, one sprang up, and stared
With piteous recognition in fixed eyes,
Lifting distressful hands as if to bless.
And by his smile, I knew that sullen hall,
By his dead smile I knew we stood in Hell.
With a thousand pains that vision's face was grained;
Yet no blood reached there from the upper ground,
And no guns thumped, or down the flues made moan.
'Strange friend,' I said, 'here is no cause to mourn.'
'None,' said that other, 'save the undone years,
The hopelessness. Whatever hope is yours,
Was my life also; I went hunting wild
After the wildest beauty in the world,
Which lies not calm in eyes, or braided hair,
But mocks the steady running of the hour,
And if it grieves, grieves richlier than here.
For of my glee might many men have laughed,
And of my weeping something had been left,
Which must die now. I mean the truth untold,
The pity of war, the pity war distilled.
Now men will go content with what we spoiled,
Or, discontent, boil bloody, and be spilled.
They will be swift with swiftness of the tigress.
None will break ranks, though nations trek from progress.
Courage was mine, and I had mystery,
Wisdom was mine, and I had mastery:
To miss the march of this retreating world
Into vain citadels that are not walled.
Then, when much blood had clogged their chariot-wheels,
I would go up and wash them from sweet wells,

Even with truths that lie too deep for taint.
I would have poured my spirit without stint
But not through wounds; not on the cess of war.
Foreheads of men have bled where no wounds were.
I am the enemy you killed, my friend.
I knew you in this dark: for so you frowned
Yesterday through me as you jabbed and killed.
I parried; but my hands were loath and cold.
Let us sleep now . . .'

J. GRIFFYTH FAIRFAX

The Forest of the Dead

There are strange trees in that pale field
Of barren soil and bitter yield:
They stand without the city walls;
Their nakedness is unconcealed.

Cross after cross, mound after mound,
And no flowers blossom but are bound,
The dying and the dead, in the wreaths,
Sad crowns for kings of Underground.

The forest of the dead is still,
No song of birds can ever thrill
Among the sapless boughs that bear
No fruit, no flower, for good or ill.

The sun by day, the moon by night
Give terrible or tender light,
But night or day the forest stands
Unchanging, desolately bright.

With loving or unloving eye
Kinsman and alien pass them by:
Do the dead know, do the dead care,
Under the forest as they lie?

To each the tree above his head,
To each the sign in which is said . . .
'By this thou art to overcome':
Under this forest sleep no dead.

These, having life, gave life away:
Is God less generous than they?
The spirit passes and is free:
Dust to the dust; Death takes the clay.

G.K. CHESTERTON

For a War Memorial

The hucksters haggle in the mart
The cars and carts go by;
Senates and schools go droning on;
For dead things cannot die.

A storm stooped on the place of tombs
With bolts to blast and rive;
But these be names of many men
The lightning found alive.

If usurers rule and rights decay
And visions view once more
Great Carthage like a golden shell
Gape hollow on the shore,

Still to the last of crumbling time
Upon this stone be read
How many men of England died
To prove they were not dead.

EDWARD THOMAS

Gone, Gone Again

Gone, gone again,
May, June, July,
And August gone,
Again gone by,

Not memorable
Save that I saw them go,
As past the empty quays
The rivers flow.

And now again,
In the harvest rain,
The Blenheim oranges
Fall grubby from the trees

As when I was young –
And when the lost one was here –
And when the war began
To turn young men to dung.

Look at the old house,
Outmoded, dignified,
Dark and untenanted,
With grass growing instead

Of the footsteps of life,
The friendliness, the strife;
In its beds have lain
Youth, love, age, and pain:

I am something like that;
Only I am not dead,
Still breathing and interested
In the house that is not dark: –

I am something like that:
Not one pane to reflect the sun,
For the schoolboys to throw at –
They have broken every one.

W.B. YEATS

Reprisals

Some nineteen German planes, they say,
You had brought down before you died.
We called it a good death. Today
Can ghost or man be satisfied?
Although your last exciting year
Outweighed all other years, you said,
Though battle joy may be so dear
A memory, even to the dead,
It chases other thought away,
Yet rise from your Italian tomb,
Flit to Kiltartan Cross and stay
Till certain second thoughts have come
Upon the cause you served, that we
Imagined such a fine affair:
Half-drunk or whole-mad soldiery
Are murdering your tenants there.
Men that revere your father yet
Are shot at on the open plain.
Where may new-married women sit
And suckle children now? Armed men
May murder them in passing by
Nor law nor parliament take heed.
Then close your ears with dust and lie
Among the other cheated dead.

SIEGFRIED SASSOON

On Passing the New Menin Gate

Who will remember, passing through this Gate,
The unheroic dead who fed the Guns?
Who shall absolve the foulness of their fate –,
Those doomed, conscripted, unvictorious ones?
    Crudely renewed, the Salient holds its own.
    Paid are its dim defenders by this pomp;
    Paid, with a pile of peace-complacent stone,
    The armies who endured that sullen swamp.

Here was the world's worst wound. And here with pride,
'Their name liveth for ever,' the Gateway claims.
Was ever an immolation so belied
As these intolerably nameless names?
Well might the Dead who struggled in the slime
Rise and deride this sepulchre of crime.

RUDYARD KIPLING

Mesopotamia

They shall not return to us, the resolute, the young,
    The eager and whole-hearted whom we gave:
But the men who left them thriftily to die in their own
        dung,
    Shall they come with years and honour to the grave?

They shall not return to us, the strong men coldly slain
    In sight of help denied from day to day:
But the men who edged their agonies and chid them in
        their pain,
    Are they too strong and wise to put away?

Our dead shall not return to us while Day and Night
    divide –
  Never while the bars of sunset hold.
But the idle-minded overlings who quibbled while they
    died,
  Shall they thrust for high employments as of old?

Shall we only threaten and be angry for an hour?
  When the storm is ended shall we find
How softly but how swiftly they have sidled back to power
  By the favour and contrivance of their kind?

Even while they soothe us, while they promise large
    amends,
  Even while they make a show of fear,
Do they call upon their debtors, and take counsel with their
    friends,
  To confirm and re-establish each career?

Their lives cannot repay us – their death could not undo –
  The shame that they have laid upon our race.
But the slothfulness that wasted and the arrogance that
    slew,
  Shall we leave it unabated in its place?

1917

A.E. HOUSMAN

Epitaph on an Army of Mercenaries

These, in the day when heaven was falling,
  The hour when earth's foundations fled,
Followed their mercenary calling
  And took their wages and are dead.

Their shoulders held the sky suspended;
  They stood, and earth's foundations stay;
What God abandoned, these defended,
  And saved the sum of things for pay.

EDWARD THOMAS

February Afternoon

Men heard this roar of parleying starlings, saw,
  A thousand years ago even as now,
  Black rooks with white gulls following the plough
So that the first are last until a caw
Commands that last are first again, – a law
  Which was of old when one, like me, dreamed how
  A thousand years might dust lie on his brow
Yet thus would birds do between hedge and shaw.

Time swims before me, making as a day
  A thousand years, while the broad ploughland oak
  Roars mill-like and men strike and bear the stroke
  Of war as ever, audacious or resigned,
And God still sits aloft in the array
  That we have wrought him, stone-deaf and stone-
    blind.

FORD MADOX FORD

That Exploit of Yours

I meet two soldiers sometimes here in Hell
The one, with a tear in the seat of his red pantaloons
Was stuck by a pitchfork,
Climbing a wall to steal apples.

The second has a seeming silver helmet,
Having died from the fall of his horse on some tram-lines
In Dortmund.

These two
Meeting in the vaulted and vaporous caverns of Hell
Exclaim always in identical tones:
'I at least have done my duty to Society and the Fatherland!'
It is strange how the cliché prevails . . .
For I will bet my hat that you who sent me here to Hell
Are saying the selfsame words at this very moment
Concerning that exploit of yours.

ROBERT GRAVES

Recalling War

Entrance and exit wounds are silvered clean,
The track aches only when the rain reminds.
The one-legged man forgets his leg of wood,
The one-armed man his jointed wooden arm.
The blinded man sees with his ears and hands
As much or more than once with both his eyes.
Their war was fought these twenty years ago
And now assumes the nature-look of time,
As when the morning traveller turns and views
His wild night-stumbling carved into a hill.

What, then, was war? No mere discord of flags
But an infection of the common sky
That sagged ominously upon the earth
Even when the season was the airiest May.
Down pressed the sky, and we, oppressed, thrust out
Boastful tongue, clenched fist and valiant yard.
Natural infirmities were out of mode,
For Death was young again: patron alone
Of healthy dying, premature fate-spasm.

Fear made fine bed-fellows. Sick with delight
At life's discovered transitoriness,
Our youth became all-flesh and waived the mind.
Never was such antiqueness of romance,
Such tasty honey oozing from the heart.
And old importances came swimming back –
Wine, meat, log-fires, a roof over the head,
A weapon at the thigh, surgeons at call.
Even there was a use again for God –
A word of rage in lack of meat, wine, fire,
In ache of wounds beyond all surgeoning.

War was return of earth to ugly earth,
War was foundering of sublimities,
Extinction of each happy art and faith
By which the world had still kept head in air,
Protesting logic or protesting love,
Until the unendurable moment struck –
The inward scream, the duty to run mad.

And we recall the merry ways of guns –
Nibbling the walls of factory and church
Like a child, piecrust; felling groves of trees
Like a child, dandelions with a switch.
Machine-guns rattle toy-like from a hill,
Down in a row the brave tin-soldiers fall:
A sight to be recalled in elder days
When learnedly the future we devote
To yet more boastful visions of despair.

SIEGFRIED SASSOON

Aftermath

Have you forgotten yet? . . .
For the world's events have rumbled on since those gagged days,
Like traffic checked while at the crossing of city-ways:
And the haunted gap in your mind has filled with thoughts that flow
Like clouds in the lit heaven of life; and you're a man reprieved
    to go,
Taking your peaceful share of Time, with joy to spare.
But the past is just the same – and War's a bloody game . . .
Have you forgotten yet? . . .
Look down, and swear by the slain of the War that you'll never forget.

Do you remember the dark months you held the sector at Mametz –
The nights you watched and wired and dug and piled sandbags on
    parapets?
Do you remember the rats; and the stench
Of corpses rotting in front of the front-line trench –
And dawn coming, dirty-white, and chill with a hopeless rain?
Do you ever stop and ask, 'Is it all going to happen again?'

Do you remember that hour of din before the attack –
And the anger, the blind compassion that seized and shook you then
As you peered at the doomed and haggard faces of your men?
Do you remember the stretcher-cases lurching back
With dying eyes and lolling heads – those ashen-grey
Masks of the lads who once were keen and kind and gay?

Have you forgotten yet? . . .
Look up, and swear by the green of the spring that you'll never forget.

March 1929

THOMAS HARDY

Channel Firing

That night your great guns, unawares,
Shook all our coffins as we lay,
And broke the chancel window-squares,
We thought it was the Judgement-day

And sat upright. While drearisome
Arose the howl of wakened hounds:
The mouse let fall the altar-crumb,
The worms drew back into the mounds,

The glebe cow drooled. Till God called, 'No;
It's gunnery practice out at sea
Just as before you went below;
The world is as it used to be:

'All nations striving strong to make
Red war yet redder. Mad as hatters
They do no more for Christés sake
Than you who are helpless in such matters.

'That this is not the judgement-hour
For some of them's a blessed thing,
For if it were they'd have to scour
Hell's floor for so much threatening . . .

'Ha, ha. It will be warmer when
I blow the trumpet (if indeed
I ever do; for you are men,
And rest eternal sorely need).'

So down we lay again. 'I wonder,
Will the world ever saner be',
Said one, 'than when He sent us under
In our indifferent century!'

And many a skeleton shook his head.
'Instead of preaching forty year',
My neighbour Parson Thirdly said,
'I wish I had stuck to pipes and beer.'

Again the guns disturbed the hour,
Roaring their readiness to avenge,
So far inland as Stourton Tower,
And Camelot, and starlit Stonehenge.

April, 1914

EZRA POUND

from Hugh Selwyn Mauberley

(Life and contacts)

These fought in any case,
and some believing,
          pro domo, in any case . . .

Some quick to arm,
some for adventure,
some from fear of weakness,
some from fear of censure,
some for love of slaughter, in imagination,
learning later . . .
some in fear, learning love of slaughter;
Died some, pro patria,
              non 'dulce' non 'et decor' . . .
walked eye-deep in hell
believing in old men's lies, then unbelieving
came home, home to a lie,
home to many deceits,
home to old lies and new infamy;
usury age-old and age-thick
and liars in public places.

Daring as never before, wastage as never before.
Young blood and high blood,
fair cheeks, and fine bodies;

fortitude as never before

frankness as never before,
disillusions as never told in the old days,
hysterias, trench confessions,
laughter out of dead bellies.

                    *   *   *

There died a myriad,
And of the best, among them,
For an old bitch gone in the teeth,
For a botched civilization,

Charm, smiling at the good mouth,
Quick eyes gone under earth's lid,

For two gross of broken statues,
For a few thousand battered books.

THE YEARS BETWEEN

Interlude:
'Our World in Stupor Lies'

OSBERT SITWELL

The Next War

To Sacheverell

The long war had ended.
Its miseries had grown faded.
Deaf men became difficult to talk to,
Heroes become bores.
Those alchemists
Who had converted blood into gold
Had grown elderly.
But they held a meeting,
Saying,
'We think perhaps we ought
To put up tombs
Or erect altars
To those brave lads
Who were so willingly burnt,
Or blinded,
Or maimed,
Who lost all likeness to a living thing,
Or were blown to bleeding patches of flesh
For our sakes.
It would look well.
Or we might even educate the children.'
But the richest of these wizards
Coughed gently;
And he said:
  'I have always been to the front
  – In private enterprise –,
  I yield in public spirit
  To no man.
  I think yours is a very good idea
  – A capital idea –
  And not too costly . . .

  But it seems to me

That the cause for which we fought
Is again endangered.
What more fitting memorial for the fallen
Than that their children
Should fall for the same cause?'
Rushing eagerly into the street,
The kindly old gentleman cried
To the young:
   'Will you sacrifice
   Through your lethargy
   What your fathers died to gain?
   The world must be made safe for the young!'

And the children
Went. . . .

November 1918

BERNARD GUTTERIDGE

In September 1939

The last war was my favourite picture story.
Illustrated London News bound in the study;
The German bayonet we believed still bloody

But it was just rusty. Privacy of death.
My uncle's uniform meant more than glory;
Surprise that grief should be so transitory . . .

All the predictions of adolescence had
Disposed of glory in their realist path:
There'd be no need to duck and hold your breath.

Now, looking as useless and as beautiful
As dragonflies, the plump silver balloons
Hang over London also like zany moons.

Yet from the blacked-out windows death still seems
Private, not an affair that's shared by all
The distant people, the flats, the Town Hall.

But some remember Spain and the black spots
They shouted 'Bombers' at. That memory screams
That we know as a film or in bad dreams.

Fear will alight on each like a dunce's cap
Or an unguessed disease unless death drops
Quicker than the sirens or the traffic stops.

TED HUGHES

Six Young Men

The celluloid of a photograph holds them well, —
Six young men, familiar to their friends.
Four decades that have faded and ochre-tinged
This photograph have not wrinkled the faces or the hands.
Though their cocked hats are not now fashionable,
Their shoes shine. One imparts an intimate smile,
One chews a grass, one lowers his eyes, bashful,
One is ridiculous with cocky pride –
Six months after this picture they were all dead.

All are trimmed for a Sunday jaunt. I know
That bilberried bank, that thick tree, that black wall,
Which are there yet and not changed. From where these sit
You hear the water of seven streams fall
To the roarer in the bottom, and through all
The leafy valley a rumouring of air go.
Pictured here, their expressions listen yet,
And still that valley has not changed its sound
Though their faces are four decades under the ground.

This one was shot in an attack and lay
Calling in the wire, then this one, his best friend,
Went out to bring him in and was shot too;
And this one, the very moment he was warned
From potting at tin-cans in no-man's-land,
Fell back dead with his rifle-sights shot away.
The rest, nobody knows what they came to,
But come to the worst they must have done, and held it
Closer than their hope; all were killed.

Here see a man's photograph,
The locket of a smile, turned overnight
Into the hospital of his mangled last
Agony and hours; see bundled in it
His mightier-than-a-man dead bulk and weight:

And on this one place which keeps him alive
(In his Sunday best) see fall war's worst
Thinkable flash and rending, onto his smile
Forty years rotting into soil.

That man's not more alive whom you confront
And shake by the hand, see hale, hear speak loud,
Than any of these six celluloid smiles are,
Nor prehistoric or fabulous beast more dead;
No thought so vivid as their smoking blood:
To regard this photograph might well dement,
Such contradictory permanent horrors here
Smile from the single exposure and shoulder out
One's own body from its instant and heat.

ALUN LEWIS

Autumn, 1939

The beech boles whiten in the swollen stream;
Their red leaves, shaken from the creaking boughs,
Float down the flooded meadow, half in dream,
Seen in a mirror cracked by broken vows,

Water-logged, slower, deeper, swirling down
Between the indifferent hills who also saw
Old jaundiced knights jog listlessly to town
To fight for love in some unreal war.

Black leaves are piled against the roaring weir;
Dark closes round the manor and the hut;
The dead knight moulders on his rotting bier,
And one by one the warped old casements shut.

HERBERT READ

To a Conscript of 1940

*Qui n'a pas une fois désespéré de l'honneur, ne sera
jamais un héros.   Georges Bernanos*

A soldier passed me in the freshly fallen snow,
His footsteps muffled, his face unearthly grey:
And my heart gave a sudden leap
As I gazed on a ghost of five-and-twenty years ago.

I shouted Halt! and my voice had the old accustom'd ring
And he obeyed it as it was obeyed
In the shrouded days when I too was one
Of an army of young men marching

Into the unknown. He turned towards me and I said:
'I am one of those who went before you
Five-and-twenty years ago: one of the many who never returned,
Of the many who returned and yet were dead.

We went where you are going, into the rain and the mud:
We fought as you will fight
With death and darkness and despair;
We gave what you will give – our brains and our blood.

We think we gave in vain. The world was not renewed.
There was hope in the homestead and anger in the streets,
But the old world was restored and we returned
To the dreary field and workshop, and the immemorial feud

Of rich and poor. Our victory was our defeat.
Power was retained where power had been misused
And youth was left to sweep away
The ashes that the fires had strewn beneath our feet.

But one thing we learned: there is no glory in the dead
Until the soldier wears a badge of tarnish'd braid;

There are heroes who have heard the rally and have seen
The glitter of a garland round their head.

Theirs is the hollow victory. They are deceived.
But you, my brother and my ghost, if you can go
Knowing that there is no reward, no certain use
In all your sacrifice, then honour is reprieved.

To fight without hope is to fight with grace,
The self reconstructed, the false heart repaired.'
Then I turned with a smile, and he answered my salute
As he stood against the fretted hedge, which was like
  white lace.

The New Warfare:
'Death is a Matter of Mathematics'

BARRY AMIEL

Death is a Matter of Mathematics

Death is a matter of mathematics.

It screeches down at you from dirtywhite nothingness
And your life is a question of velocity and altitude,
With allowances for wind and the quick, relentless pull
Of gravity.

Or else it lies concealed
In that fleecy, peaceful puff of cloud ahead,
A streamlined, muttering vulture, waiting
To swoop upon you with a rush of steel.
And then your chances vary as the curves
Of your parabolas, your banks, your dives,
The scientific soundness of your choice
Of what to push or pull, and how, and when.
Or perhaps you walk oblivious in a wood,
Or crawl flat-bellied over pockmarked earth,
And Death awaits you in a field-gray tunic.
Sights upright and aligned. Range estimated
And set in. A lightning, subconscious calculation
Of trajectory and deflection. With you the focal point,
The centre of the problem. The A and B
Or Smith and Jones of schoolboy textbooks.

Ten out of ten means you are dead.

HENRY REED

Judging Distances

Not only how far away, but the way that you say it
Is very important. Perhaps you may never get
The knack of judging a distance, but at least you know
How to report on a landscape: the central sector,
The right of arc and that, which we had last Tuesday,
  And at least you know

That maps are of time, not place, so far as the army
Happens to be concerned – the reason being,
Is one which need not delay us. Again, you know
There are three kinds of tree, three only, the fir and
    the poplar,
And those which have bushy tops to; and lastly
  That things only seem to be things.

A barn is not called a barn, to put it more plainly,
Or a field in the distance, where sheep may be safely
    grazing.
You must never be over-sure. You must say, when
    reporting:
At five o'clock in the central sector is a dozen
Of what appear to be animals; whatever you do,
  Don't call the bleeders *sheep*.

I am sure that's quite clear; and suppose, for the sake
    of example,
The one at the end, asleep, endeavours to tell us
What he sees over there to the west, and how far away,
After first having come to attention. There to the west,
On the fields of summer the sun and the shadows bestow
  Vestments of purple and gold.

The still white dwellings are like a mirage in the heat,
And under the swaying elms a man and a woman
Lie gently together. Which is, perhaps, only to say

That there is a row of houses to the left of arc,
And that under some poplars a pair of what appear to be
   humans
  Appear to be loving.

Well that, for an answer, is what we might rightly call
Moderately satisfactory only, the reason being,
Is that two things have been omitted, and those are
   important.
The human beings, now: in what direction are they,
And how far away, would you say? And do not forget
  There may be dead ground in between.

There may be dead ground in between: and I may not
   have got
The knack of judging a distance. I will only venture
A guess that perhaps between me and the apparent lovers,
(Who, incidentally, appear by now to have finished)
At seven o'clock from the houses, is roughly a distance
  Of about one year and a half.

ALAN ROSS

Destroyers in the Arctic

Camouflaged, they detach lengths of sea and sky
When they move; offset, speed and direction are a lie.

Everything is grey anyway; ships, water, snow, faces.
Flanking the convoy, we rarely go through our paces:

But sometimes on tightening waves at night they wheel
Drawing white moons on strings from dripping keel.

Cold cases them, like ships in glass; they are formal,
Not real, except in adversity. Then, too, have to seem normal.

At dusk they intensify dusk, strung out, non-committal:
Waves spill from our wake, crêpe paper magnetized by gun-metal.

They breathe silence, less solid than ghosts, ruminative
As the Arctic breaks up on their sides and they sieve

Moisture into mess-decks. Heat is cold-lined there,
Where we wait for a torpedo and lack air.

Repetitive of each other, imitating the sea's lift and fall,
On the wings of the convoy they indicate rehearsal.

Merchantmen move sideways, with the gait of crustaceans,
Round whom like eels escorts take up their stations.

Landfall, Murmansk; but starboard now a lead-coloured
Island, Jan Mayen. Days identical, hoisted like sails, blurred.

Counters moved on an Admiralty map, snow like confetti
Covers the real us. We dream we are counterfeits tied to our jetty.

But cannot dream long; the sea curdles and sprawls,
Liverishly real, and merciless all else away from us falls.

GAVIN EWART

The Bofors AA Gun

Such marvellous ways to kill a man!
An 'instrument of precision', a beauty,
The well-oiled shining marcel of our day
Points an accusing finger at the sky.
– But suddenly, traversing, elevating madly,
It plunges into action, more than eager
For the steel blood of those romantic birds
That threaten all the towns and roads.
O, that man's ingenuity, in this so subtle,
In such harmonious synchronisation of parts,
Should against man be turned and be complaisant,
The pheasant-shooter be himself the pheasant!

JOHN GILLESPIE MAGEE, Jr

High Flight

Oh, I have slipped the surly bonds of earth,
And danced the skies on laughter-silvered wings;
Sunward I've climbed and joined the tumbling mirth
Of sun-split clouds – and done a hundred things
You have not dreamed of – wheeled and soared and swung
High in the sunlit silence. Hov'ring there,
I've chased the shouting wind along and flung
My eager craft through footless halls of air.
Up, up the long delirious, burning blue
I've topped the wind-swept heights with easy grace,
Where never lark, or even eagle, flew;
And, while with silent, lifting mind I've trod
The high untrespassed sanctity of space,
Put out my hand, and touched the face of God.

RANDALL JARRELL

A Front

Fog over the base: the beams ranging
From the five towers pull home from the night
The crews cold in fur, the bombers banging
Like lost trucks down the levels of the ice.
A glow drifts in like mist (how many tons of it?),
Bounces to a roll, turns suddenly to steel
And tires and turrets, huge in the trembling light.
The next is high, and pulls up with a wail,
Comes round again – no use. And no use for the rest
In drifting circles out along the range;
Holding no longer, changed to a kinder course,
The flights drone southward through the steady rain.
The base is closed. . . . But one voice keeps on calling,
The lowering pattern of the engines grows;
The roar gropes downward in its shaky orbit
For the lives the season quenches. Here below
They beg, order, are not heard; and hear the darker
Voice rising: *Can't you hear me? Over. Over –*
All the air quivers, and the east sky glows.

R.N. CURREY

Unseen Fire

This is a damned inhuman sort of war.
I have been fighting in a dressing-gown
Most of the night; I cannot see the guns,
The sweating gun-detachments or the planes;

I sweat down here before a symbol thrown
Upon a screen, sift facts, initiate
Swift calculations and swift orders; wait
For the precise split-second to order fire.

We chant our ritual words; beyond the phones
A ghost repeats the orders to the guns:
One Fire . . . Two Fire . . . ghosts answer: the guns roar
Abruptly; and an aircraft waging war
Inhumanly from nearly five miles height
Meets our bouquet of death—and turns sharp right.

RICHARD EBERHART

Dam Neck, Virginia

Anti-aircraft seen from a certain distance
On a steely blue night say a mile away
Flowers on the air absolutely dream-like,
The vision has no relation to the reality.

The floating balls of light are tossed easily
And float out into space without a care,
They the sailors of the gentlest parabolas
In a companionship and with a kind of stare.

They are a controlled kind of falling stars,
But not falling, rising and floating and going out,
Teaming together in efflorescent spectacle
Seemingly better than nature's: man is on the lookout.

The men are firing tracers, practising at night.
Each specialist himself precision's instrument.
These expert prestidigitators press the luminence
In knowledge of and ignorance of their doing.

They do not know the dream-like vision ascending
In me, one mile away: they had not thought of that.
Huddled in darkness behind their bright projectors
They are the scientists of the skill to kill.

As this sight and show is gentle and false,
The truth of guns is fierce that aims at death.
Of war in the animal sinews let us speak not,
But of the beautiful disrelation of the spiritual.

KEITH DOUGLAS

How to Kill

Under the parabòla of a ball,
a child turning into a man,
I looked into the air too long.
The ball fell in my hand, it sang
in the closed fist: *Open Open*
Behold a gift designed to kill.

Now in my dial of glass appears
the soldier who is going to die.
He smiles, and moves about in ways
his mother knows, habits of his.
The wires touch his face: I cry
NOW. Death, like a familiar, hears

and look, has made a man of dust
of a man of flesh. This sorcery
I do. Being dammed, I am amused
to see the centre of love diffused
and the waves of love travel into vacancy.
How easy it is to make a ghost.

The weightless mosquito touches
her tiny shadow on the stone,
and with how like, how infinite
a lightness, man and shadow meet.
They fuse. A shadow is a man
when the mosquito death approaches.

Lamentations:
'The Rock of Grief'

SIDNEY KEYES

Advice for a Journey

The drums mutter for war, and soon we must begin
To seek the country where they say that joy
Springs flowerlike among the rocks, to win
The fabulous golden mountain of our peace.

O my friends, we are too young
To be explorers, have no skill nor compass,
Nor even that iron certitude which swung
Our fathers at their self-fulfilling North.

So take no rations, remember not your homes –
Only the blind and stubborn hope to track
This wilderness. The thoughtful leave their bones
In windy foodless meadows of despair.

Never look back, nor too far forward search
For the white Everest of your desire;
The screes roll underfoot, and you will never reach
Those brittle peaks which only clouds may walk.

Others have come before you, and immortal
Live like reflections. Their still faces
Will give you courage to ignore the subtle
Sneer of the gentian and the iceworn pebble.

The fifes cry death and the sharp winds call.
Set your face to the rock; go on, go out
Into the bad lands of battle, the cloud-wall
Of the future, my friends, and leave your fear.

Go forth, my friends, the raven is no sibyl;
Break the clouds' anger with your unchanged faces.
You'll find, maybe, the dream under the hill –
But never Canaan, nor any golden mountain.

ALUN LEWIS

Infantry

By day these men ask nothing, and obey;
They eat their bread behind a heap of stones;
Hardship and violence grow an easy way,
Winter is like a girl within their bones.

They learn the gambits of the soul,
Think lightly of the themes of life and death,
All mortal anguish shrunk into an ache
Too nagging to be worth the catch of breath.

Sharing Life's iron rations, marching light,
Enduring to the end the early cold,
The emptiness of noon, the void of night
In whose black market they are bought and sold;
They take their silent stations for the fight
Rum's holy unction makes the dubious bold.

1945

RANDALL JARRELL

The Dead Wingman

Seen on the sea, no sign; no sign, no sign
In the black firs and terraces of hills
Ragged in mist. The cone narrows, snow
Glares from the bleak walls of a crater. No.
Again the houses jerk like paper, turn,
And the surf streams by: a port of toys
Is starred with its fires and faces; but no sign.

In the level light, over the fiery shores,
The plane circles stubbornly: the eyes distending
With hatred and misery and longing, stare

Over the blackening ocean for a corpse.
The fires are guttering; the dials fall,
A long dry shudder climbs along his spine,
His fingers tremble; but his hard unchanging stare
Moves unacceptingly: *I have a friend.*

The fires are grey; no star, no sign
Winks from the breathing darkness of the carrier
Where the pilot circles for his wingman; where,
Gliding above the cities' shells, a stubborn eye
Among the embers of the nations, achingly
Tracing the circles of that worn, unchanging No –
The lives' long war, lost war – the pilot sleeps.

KEITH DOUGLAS

Enfidaville

In the church fallen like dancers
lie the Virgin and St Thérèse
on little pillows of dust.
The detonations of the last few days
tore down the ornamental plasters
shivered the hands of Christ.

The men and women who moved like candles
in and out of the houses and the streets
are all gone. The white houses are bare
black cages. No one is left to greet
the ghosts tugging at doorhandles
opening doors that are not there.

Now the daylight coming in from the fields
like a labourer, tired and sad,
is peering about among the wreckage, goes
past some corners as though with averted head
not looking at the pain this town holds,
seeing no one move behind the windows.

But already they are coming back; to search
like ants, poking in the débris, finding in it
a bed or a piano and carrying it out.
Who would not love them at this minute?
I seem again to meet
The blue eyes of the images in the church.

DRUMMOND ALLISON

A Funeral Oration

For Douglas whom the cloud and eddy rejected,
Though glad in dark Wellington he had deserved
Perpetual fellowship with those aerish beasts
Whom the eloquent eagle introduced to Chaucer;
But now the North Sea separates his bones
– Douglas who cocked an incessant snook at Death –
And crab and plaice make love wherever his soul
Shrived by a Messerschmidt cannon began to be sand,
They make light of his non-watertight prowess.

For Robert whom the wrath of the Atlantic
And untiring fire proved by the mouth of the River
Plate, but later the Mediterranean
Whose vaults he visited tricked and shut securely
In, and he penetrates forever the palaces of Atlantis.

For Colin last seen within sight of Greenland,
Who disagreed with all the gods and went down
The gradual stairs of the sea with the *Hood* until
He could have used vacated shells for tankards
A vigorous white worm for a cigarette
And girl friends having swords upon their snouts.

DAVID GASCOYNE

De Profundis

Out of these depths:

Where footsteps wander in the marsh of death and an
Intense infernal glare is on our faces facing down:

Out of these depths, what shamefaced cry
Half choked in the dry throat, as though a stone
Were our confounded tongue, can ever rise:
Because the mind has been struck blind
And may no more conceive
Thy Throne.

Because the depths
Are clear with only death's
Marsh-light, because the rock of grief
Is clearly too extreme for us to breach:
Deepen our depths,

And aid our unbelief.

G.S. FRASER

Lament

In a dismal air; a light of breaking summer
Under the conspicuous dolour of a leaden sky,
We walk by the river, beneath the deciduous branches;
Cold in the water the webs of the cold light lie.

Always the sky bleeds with sorrow that no light stanches
In the evenings of autumn, when rust coloured crisp leaves fly,
Always the heart is uneasy and full of foreboding:
Always the heart is uneasy and cannot tell why.

Always the rust of the leaves and the light is corroding
The steel of the evening, gun-metal blue of the sky.
Always the river is lisping and lapping of sorrow.
Like the leaves and the light, the incontinent impulses die.

No more appointments to meet and continue tomorrow.
No more postponements of parting, with hesitant sigh.
Here's the great year in its circle, announcing departure.
Here are your hard lips on mine and goodbye and goodbye.

Summer resumes the occasion but not the adventure.
Always the heart is uneasy and cannot tell why.
In a dismal air; a light of breaking summer,
Cold in the water the webs of the cold light lie.

CHARLES CAUSLEY

At the British War Cemetery, Bayeux

I walked where in their talking graves
And shirts of earth five thousand lay,
When history with ten feasts of fire
Had eaten the red air away.

I am Christ's boy, I cried, I bear
In iron hands the bread, the fishes.
I hang with honey and with rose
This tidy wreck of all your wishes.

On your geometry of sleep
The chestnut and the fir-tree fly,
And lavender and marguerite
Forge with their flowers an English sky.

Turn now toward the belling town
Your jigsaws of impossible bone,
And rising read your rank of snow
Accurate as death upon the stone.

About your easy heads my prayers
I said with syllables of clay.
What gift, I asked, shall I bring now
Before I weep, and walk away?

Take, they replied, the oak and laurel.
Take our fortune of tears and live
Like a spendthrift lover. All we ask
Is the one gift you cannot give.

HENRY TREECE

Three Pleas

Stand by me, Death, lest these dark days
Should hurt me more than I may know;
I beg that if the wound grows sharp
You take me when I ask to go.

Step closer, Love, and dry your tears,
What's marred you'll never mend by tears;
Let's finish where the tale began
And kiss away the ruined years.

A moment, Faith, before you leave,
There's one last favour I would ask;
Put to some use your handsome hand
And show me the face behind your mask.

ALUN LEWIS

The Sentry

I have begun to die.
For now at last I know
That there is no escape
From Night. Not any dream
Nor breathless images of sleep
Touch my bat's-eyes. I hang
Leathery-arid from the hidden roof
Of Night, and sleeplessly
I watch within Sleep's province.
I have left
The lovely bodies of the boy and girl
Deep in each other's placid arms;
And I have left
The beautiful lanes of sleep
That barefoot lovers follow to this last
Cold shore of thought I guard.
I have begun to die
And the guns' implacable silence
Is my black interim, my youth and age,
In the flower of fury, the folded poppy,
Night.

ANTHONY RICHARDSON

Song to Hymen: 1942

My friend's sweet love came into town,
With a new gay air and a gay new gown;
We drank at the inn, before he led
His glad girl-bride to their wedding bed.

His lady left and her gown was black,
She never smiled, nor glanced she back,
And she threw as she passed, on a heap of stone,
The key of a room that love had known.

ROY FULLER

The Middle of a War

My photograph already looks historic.
The promising youthful face, the matelot's collar,
Say 'This one is remembered for a lyric.
His place and period – nothing could be duller.'

Its position is already indicated –
The son or brother in the album; pained
The expression and the garments dated,
His fate so obviously pre-ordained.

The original turns away; as horrible thoughts,
Loud fluttering aircraft slope above his head
At dusk. The ridiculous empires break like biscuits.

Ah, life has been abandoned by the boats –
Only the trodden island and the dead
Remain, and the once inestimable caskets.

WORLD WAR TWO

In Foreign Parts:
'The Maps Mock Us'

LINCOLN KIRSTEIN

P.O.E.

THIS IS IT and so: so long.
  We're soldiers now, all set to sail.
We may not sing one sad old song
  Herded within a dark dock-rail.

Self-pity pools its furtive tear;
  Expect the Worst, discount the Best.
Insurance as a form of fear
  Tickles the terror in each chest.

So: THIS IS IT—and yet not the sheer
  Crude crisis we've been trained to take,
For many a female volunteer
  Doles out thin cocoa with thick cake.

They've parked their limousines the while;
  Their natty uniform is spick
And span, their hairdo and their smile
  Pronounces patriotic chic;

And THIS IS IT for these dames too.
  We strive to fake a grateful note
But goddam duffel bag and pack,
  Gas mask, rifle, helmet, coat

Too heavy are, so each sad sack
  Must flop and gripe: This is *some* shit.
Up On Your Feet, our orders crack.
  It's All Aboard for THIS IS IT.

ROY FULLER

In Africa

Parabolas of grief, the hills are never
Hills and the plains,
Where through the torrid air the lions shiver,
No longer plains.

Just as the lives of lions now are made
Shabby with rifles,
This great geography shrinks into sad
And personal trifles.

For those who are in love and are exiled
Can never discover
How to be happy: looking upon the wild
They see for ever

The cultivated acre of their pain;
The clouds like dreams,
Involved, improbable; the endless plain,
Precisely as it seems.

ALUN LEWIS

The Peasants

The dwarf barefooted, chanting
Behind the oxen by the lake,
Stepping lightly and lazily among the thorntrees
Dusky and dazed with sunlight, half awake;

The women breaking stones upon the highway,
Walking erect with burdens on their heads,
One body growing in another body,
Creation touching verminous straw beds.

Across scorched hills and trampled crops
The soldiers straggle by.
History staggers in their wake.
The peasants watch them die.

R.N. CURREY

Burial Flags

Here with the desert so austere that only
Flags live, plant out your flags upon the wind,
Red tattered bannerets that mark a lonely
    Grave in the sand;

A crude oblong of stone to hold some mortal
Remains against a jackal's rooting paws,
Painted with colour-wash to look like marble
    Through the heat-haze;

Roofed casually with corrugated iron
Held up by jutting and uneven poles;
The crooked flagpoles tied to a curved headstone
    Carved with symbols –

Stars and new moon that are the only flowers
To grow out of this naked earth and sky,
Except these flags that through the windy hours
    Bloom steadily,

Dull red, the faded red of women's garments
Carried on sudden camels past the sky –
Red strips of cloth that ride the dusty heavens
    Untiringly.

KEITH DOUGLAS

Cairo Jag

Shall I get drunk or cut myself a piece of cake,
a pasty Syrian with a few words of English
or the Turk who says she is a princess – she dances
apparently by levitation? Or Marcelle, Parisienne
always preoccupied with her dull dead lover:
she has all the photographs and his letters
tied in a bundle and stamped *Décédé* in mauve ink.
All this takes place in a stink of jasmin.

But there are the streets dedicated to sleep
stenches and sour smells, the sour cries
do not disturb their application to slumber
all day, scattered on the pavement like rags
afflicted with fatalism and hashish. The women
offering their children brown-paper breasts
dry and twisted, elongated like the skull,
Holbein's signature. But this stained white town
is something in accordance with mundane conventions –
Marcelle drops her Gallic airs and tragedy
suddenly shrieks in Arabic about the fare
with the cabman, links herself so
with the somnambulists and legless beggars:
it is all one, all as you have heard.

But by a day's travelling you reach a new world
the vegetation is of iron
dead tanks, gun barrels split like celery
the metal brambles have no flowers or berries
and there are all sorts of manure, you can imagine
the dead themselves, their boots, clothes and possessions
clinging to the ground, a man with no head
has a packet of chocolate and a souvenir of Tripoli.

RANDALL JARRELL

A Camp in the Prussian Forest

I walk beside the prisoners to the road.
Load on puffed load,
Their corpses, stacked like sodden wood,
Lie barred or galled with blood.

By the charred warehouse. No one comes today
In the old way
To knock the fillings from their teeth;
The dark, coned, common wreath

Is plaited for their grave – a kind of grief.
The living leaf
Clings to the planted profitable
Pine if it is able;

The boughs sigh, mile on green, calm, breathing mile,
From this dead file
The planners ruled for them. . . . One year
They sent a million here:

Here men were drunk like water, burnt like wood.
The fat of good
And evil, the breast's star of hope
Were rendered into soap.

I paint the star I sawed from yellow pine –
And plant the sign
In soil that does not yet refuse
Its usual Jews

Their first asylum. But the white, dwarfed star –
This dead white star –
Hides nothing, pays for nothing; smoke
Fouls it, a yellow joke,

The needles of the wreath are chalked with ash,
A filmy trash
Litters the black woods with the death
Of men; and one last breath

Curls from the monstrous chimney . . . I laugh aloud
Again and again;
The star laughs from its rotting shroud
Of flesh. O star of men!

G.S. FRASER

Rostov

That year they fought in the snow
On the enormous plain, the rivulets
Thick with the yellow thaw, and darker, dark
With what at distance might be blood or shadows:
Everything melted, everything numbed, broke,
Every hand was pawing at desolation
And the huge stupid machine felt a shudder.
It did not matter about all the dead
For what better than death in battle
(The sick voice said in the belly,
'What better than death in battle?')
And the heart had been numbed long ago
Against particular pity (yes, and some,
And some have had their pact against all pity:
'If we ask mercy, let it be counted weakness,
And if we repent, let it be counted strategy!').

But the artillery in its tremendous
Asseveration of another existence
Was like the mask of Lenin, thundering power
From a controlled centre. And lumbering
Came the great new tanks, and always
The artillery kept saying, 'You make
An effort but it exhausts itself,
Everything meets its shock.' And some

Seemed to hear in its thunder, just
The syllables of that strong man, 'They want
A war of extermination, let them have it!'
And there was always blinding and stupefying
The snow, the wet, shivering soddenness:
And a purpose against one roused that meant death.

So the thing began to stagger, lumbering back,
Reeling under these statements, propositions,
The oratory of the last argument death:
Hammering, hammering, hammering home,
'One man is like another, one strength
Like another strength, and the wicked
Shall not prosper forever, and the turns
Of history bring the innocent to victory':
The guns lashing like Churchill's sentences
Or the blows of a whip.

The terrible strength of Tolstoy,
And Dostoevsky's vision, Lenin's silences,
The great, crude, broad-thewed man with innocent eye
Standing like a queer rock in the path:
And lashing death like lightings from the heavens.

That year it had rained death like apples,
That year the wicked were strong. But remember
That the time comes when the thing that you strike
Rouses itself, suddenly, very terribly,
And stands staring with a terribly patient look
And says, 'Why do you strike me, brother? I am Man.'

HAMISH HENDERSON

End of a Campaign

There are many dead in the brutish desert,
    who lie uneasy
among the scrub in this landscape of half-wit
stunted ill-will. For the dead land is insatiate
and necrophilous. The sand is blowing about still.
Many who for various reasons, or because
    of mere unanswerable compulsion, came here
and fought among the clutching gravestones,
    shivered and sweated,
cried out, suffered thirst, were stoically silent, cursed
the spittering machine-guns, were homesick for Europe
and fast embedded in quicksand of Africa
    agonized and died.
And sleep now. Sleep here the sleep of the dust.

There were our own, there were the others.
Their deaths were like their lives, human and animal.
There were no gods and precious few heroes.
What they regretted when they died had nothing to do
    with race and leader, realm indivisible,
laboured Augustan speeches or vague imperial heritage.
(They saw through that guff before the axe fell.)
    Their longing turned to
the lost world glimpsed in the memory of letters:
an evening at the pictures in the friendly dark,
two knowing conspirators smiling and whispering secrets;
    or else
a family gathering in the homely kitchen
with Mum so proud of her boys in uniform:
    their thoughts trembled
between moments of estrangement, and ecstatic moments
of reconciliation: and their desire
crucified itself against the unutterable shadow of someone
whose photo was in their wallets.
Then death made his incision.

There were our own, there were the others.
Therefore, minding the great word of Glencoe's
son, that we should not disfigure ourselves
with villainy of hatred; and seeing that all
have gone down like curs into anonymous silence,
I will bear witness for I knew the others.
Seeing that littoral and interior are alike indifferent
and the birds are drawn again to our welcoming north
why should I not sing them, the dead, the innocent?

ALUN LEWIS

The Mahratta Ghats

The valleys crack and burn, the exhausted plains
Sink their black teeth into the horny veins
Straggling the hills' red thighs, the bleating goats
– Dry bents and bitter thistles in their throats –
Thread the loose rocks by immemorial tracks.
Dark peasants drag the sun upon their backs.

High on the ghat the new turned soil is red,
The sun has ground it to the finest red,
It lies like gold within each horny hand.
Siva has spilt his seed upon this land.

Will she who burns and withers on the plain
Leave, ere too late, her scraggy herds of pain,
The cow-dung fire and the trembling beasts,
The little wicked gods, the grinning priests,
And climb, before a thousand years have fled,
High as the eagle to her mountain bed
Whose soil is fine as flour and blood-red?

But no! She cannot move. Each arid patch
Owns the lean folk who plough and scythe and thatch
Its grudging yield and scratch its stubborn stones.
The small gods suck the marrow from their bones.

Who is it climbs the summit of the road?
Only the beggar bumming his dark load.
Who was it cried to see the falling star?
Only the landless soldier lost in war.

And did a thousand years go by in vain?
And does another thousand start again?

BERNARD GUTTERIDGE

Shillong

I crowd all earth into a traveller's eye
Fragment by fragment. Only he
Can see the withering scar or sublime flower
For the first time joined in his own hour.

The market strewn with gutted fish; and fruit
Spewed open for the kites; the cries
And foul and sultry smell. A revered priest
Stooping in ashes: the greatest, the least.

Testing North towards Tibet the cold
Austere horizon of coarse green pines
Holds trapped the waterfall. The wide sky throws
White clouds towards the annihilating snows.

SIDNEY KEYES

The Wilderness

The red rock wilderness
Shall be my dwelling-place.

Where the wind saws at the bluffs
And the pebble falls like thunder
I shall watch the clawed sun
Tear the rocks asunder.

The seven-branched cactus
Will never sweat wine:
My own bleeding feet
Shall furnish the sign.

The rock says 'Endure.'
The wind says 'Pursue.'
The sun says 'I will suck your bones
And afterwards bury you.'

Total War:
'All the World is Terrible'

JOHN JARMAIN

Embarkation, 1942

In undetected trains we left our land
At evening secretly, from wayside stations.
None knew our place of parting; no pale hand
Waved as we went, not one friend said farewell.
But grouped on weed-grown platforms
Only a few officials holding watches
Noted the stealthy hour of our departing,
And, as we went, turned back to their hotel.
With blinds drawn down we left the things we know,
The simple fields, the homely ricks and yards;
Passed willows greyly bunching to the moon
And English towns. But in our blindfold train
Already those were far and long ago,
Stored quiet pictures which the mind must keep:
We saw them not. Instead we played at cards,
Or strangely dropped asleep.

Then in a callow dawn we stood in lines
Like foreigners on bare and unknown quays,
Till someone bravely into the hollow of waiting
Cast a timid wisp of song;
It moved along the lines of patient soldiers
Like a secret passed from mouth to mouth
And slowly gave us ease;
In our whispered singing courage was set free,
We were banded once more and strong.
So we sang as our ship set sail,
Sang our own songs, and leaning on the rail
Waved to the workmen on the slipping quay
And they again to us for fellowship.

EDWIN MUIR

The Interrogation

We could have crossed the road but hesitated,
And then came the patrol:
The leader conscientious and intent,
The men surly, indifferent.
While we stood by and waited
The interrogation began. He says the whole
Must come out now, who, what we are,
Where we have come from, with what purpose, whose
Country or camp we plot for or betray.
Question on question.
We have stood and answered through the standing day
And watched across the road beyond the hedge
The careless lovers in pairs go by,
Hand linked in hand, wandering another star,
So near we could shout to them. We cannot choose
Answer or action here,
Though still the careless lovers saunter by
And the thoughtless field is near.
We are on the very edge,
Endurance almost done,
And still the interrogation is going on.

SIDNEY KEYES

The Expected Guest

The table is spread, the lamp glitters and sighs;
Light on my eyes, light on the high curved iris
And springing from glaze to steel, from cup to knife
Makes sacramental my poor midnight table,
My broken scraps the pieces of a god.

O when they bore you down, the grinning soldiers,

Was it their white teeth you could not forget?
And when you met the beast in the myrtle wood,
When the spear broke and the blood broke out on
    your side,
What Syrian Veronica above you
Stooped with her flaxen cloth as yet unsigned?
And either way, how could you call your darling
To drink the cup of blood your father filled?

We are dying tonight, you in the aged darkness
and I in the white room my pride has rented.
And either way, we have to die alone.

The laid table stands hard and white as tomorrow.
The lamp sings. The West wind jostles the door.
Though broken the bread, the brain, the brave body
There cannot now be any hope of changing
The leavings to living bone, the bone to bread:
For bladed centuries are drawn between us.
The room is ready, but the guest is dead.

ALUN LEWIS

Goodbye

So we must say Goodbye, my darling,
And go, as lovers go, for ever;
Tonight remains, to pack and fix on labels
And make an end of lying down together.

I put a final shilling in the gas,
And watch you slip your dress below your knees
And lie so still I hear your rustling comb
Modulate the autumn in the trees.

And all the countless things I shall remember
Lay mummy-cloths of silence round my head;
I fill the carafe with a drink of water;
You say 'We paid a guinea for this bed,'

And then, 'We'll leave some gas, a little warmth
For the next resident, and these dry flowers,'
And turn your face away, afraid to speak
The big word, that Eternity is ours.

Your kisses close my eyes and yet you stare
As though God struck a child with nameless fears;
Perhaps the water glitters and discloses
Time's chalice and its limpid useless tears.

Everything we renounce except our selves;
Selfishness is the last of all to go;
Our sighs are exhalations of the earth,
Our footprints leave a track across the snow.

We made the universe to be our home,
Our nostrils took the wind to be our breath,
Our hearts are massive towers of delight,
We stride across the seven seas of death.

Yet when all's done you'll keep the emerald
I placed upon your finger in the street;
And I will keep the patches that you sewed
On my old battledress tonight, my sweet.

RANDALL JARRELL

Eighth Air Force

If, in an odd angle of the hutment,
A puppy laps the water from a can
Of flowers, and the drunk sergeant shaving
Whistles O *Paradiso!* – shall I say that man
Is not as men have said: a wolf to man?

The other murderers troop in yawning;
Three of them play Pitch, one sleeps, and one
Lies counting missions, lies there sweating
Till even his heart beats: One; One; One.
O *murderers!* . . . Still, this is how it's done.

This is a war . . . But since these play, before they die,
Like puppies with their puppy: since, a man,
I did as these have done, but did not die –
I will content the people as I can
And give up these to them: Behold the man!

I have suffered, in a dream, because of him,
Many things; for this last saviour, man,
I have lied as I lie now. But what is lying?
Men wash their hands, in blood, as best they can:
I find no fault in this just man.

ROY FULLER

What is Terrible

Life at last I know is terrible:
The innocent scene, the innocent walls and light
And hills for me are like the cavities
Of surgery or dreams. The visible might
Vanish, for all it reassures, in white.

This apprehension has come slowly to me,
Like symptoms and bulletins of sickness. I
Must first be moved across two oceans, then
Bored, systematically and sickeningly,
In a place where war is news. And constantly

I must be threatened with what is certainly worse:
Peril and death, but no less boring. And
What else? Besides my fear, my misspent time,
My love, hurt and postponed, there is the hand
Moving the empty glove; the bland

Aspect of nothing disguised as something; that
Part of living incommunicable,
For which we try to find vague adequate
Images, and which, after all,
Is quite surprisingly communicable.

Because in the clear hard light of war the ghosts
Are seen to be suspended by wires, and in
The old house the attic is empty: and the furious
Inner existence of objects and even
Ourselves is largely a myth: and for the sin

To blame our fathers, to attribute vengeance
To the pursuing chorus, and to live
In a good and tenuous world of private values,
Is simply to lie when only truth can give
Continuation in time to bread and love.

For what is terrible is the obvious
Organization of life: the oiled black gun,
And what it cost, the destruction of Europe by
Its councils; the unending justification
Of that which cannot be justified, what is done.

The year, the month, the day, the minute, at war
Is terrible and my participation
And that of all the world is terrible.
My living now must bear the laceration
Of the herd, and always will. What's done

To me is done to many. I can see
No ghosts, but only the fearful actual
Lives of my comrades. If the empty whitish
Horror is ever to be flushed and real,
It must be for them and changed by them all.

GEORGE BARKER

To my Mother

Most near, most dear, most loved and most far,
Under the window where I often found her
Sitting as huge as Asia, seismic with laughter,
Gin and chicken helpless in her Irish hand,
Irresistible as Rabelais, but most tender for
The lame dogs and hurt birds that surround her, –
She is a procession no one can follow after
But be like a little dog following a brass band.

She will not glance up at the bomber, or condescend
To drop her gin and scuttle to a cellar,
But lean on the mahogany table like a mountain
Whom only faith can move, and so I send
O all my faith and all my love to tell her
That she will move from mourning into morning.

ALAN ROSS

Mess Deck

The bulkhead sweating, and under naked bulbs
Men writing letters, playing Ludo. The light
Cuts their arms off at the wrist, only the dice
Lives. Hammocks swing, nuzzling-in tight
Like foals into flanks of mares. Bare shoulders
Glisten with oil, tattoo-marks rippling their scales on
Mermaids or girls' thighs as dice are shaken, cards played.
We reach for sleep like a gas, randy for oblivion.
But, laid out on lockers, some get waylaid;
And lie stiff, running off films in the mind's dark-room.
The air soupy, yet still cold; a beam sea rattles
Cups smelling of stale tea, knocks over a broom.
The light is watery, like the light of the sea-bed;
Marooned in it, stealthy as fishes, we may even be dead.

DESMOND HAWKINS

Night Raid

The sleepers humped down on the benches,
The daft boy was playing rummy with anyone he could get,
And the dancing girl said, 'What I say is,
If there's a bomb made for YOU,
You're going to get it.'
Someone muttered, 'The bees are coming again.'
Someone whispered beside me in the darkness,
'They're coming up from the east.'
Way off the guns muttered distantly.

This was in the small hours, at the ebb.
And the dancing girl clicked her teeth like castanets
And said, 'I don't mind life, believe me.
I like it. If there's any more to come,
I can take it and be glad of it.'
She was shivering and laughing and throwing her head back.
On the pavement men looked up thoughtfully,
Making plausible conjectures. The night sky
Throbbed under the cool bandage of the searchlights.

LOUIS SIMPSON

A Story about Chicken Soup

In my grandmother's house there was always chicken soup
And talk of the old country – mud and boards,
Poverty,
The snow falling down the necks of lovers.

Now and then, out of her savings
She sent them a dowry. Imagine
The rice-powdered faces!
And the smell of the bride, like chicken soup.

But the Germans killed them
I know it's in bad taste to say it,
But it's true. The Germans killed them all.

      *   *   *

In the ruins of Berchtesgaden
A child with yellow hair
Ran out of a doorway.

A German girl-child –
Cuckoo, all skin and bones –
Not even enough to make chicken soup.
She sat by the stream and smiled.

Then as we splashed in the sun
She laughed at us.
We had killed her mechanical brothers,
So we forgave her.

      *   *   *

The sun is shining.
The shadows of the lovers have disappeared.
They are all eyes; they have some demand on me –
They want me to be more serious than I want to be.

They want me to stick in their mudhole
Where no one is elegant.
They want me to wear old clothes,
They want me to be poor, to sleep in a room
    with many others –

Not to walk in the painted sunshine
To a summer house,
But to live in the tragic world forever.

LINCOLN KIRSTEIN

Gripe

Who is a friend? Who is a foe?
    No answer's absolutely clear
But every sign intends to show
    Friends are Up Front; foes To the Rear.
Our own troops, forward – limp or stiff
    At every shell that they sense shot –
Sorta react like we would if
    We were Up with them. We are not.
Safe back, I'll curse my colonel's name
    Whose whimsy aggravates my life;
Griping's an intellectual game
    Absolving me from guilt or strife.
I'll not desert my desk secure
    No cede it to some combat man
Whose ruggeder nature shall endure
    A larger love, a shorter span.

Yet should one wander six miles west
    Where mortar barrage splinters night,
I could relieve two for a rest
    Pondering friendship, pluck, or fright.

In a charred stable, on damp grain
    Shock slaughtered cows shan't want to eat,
Shiver twin jokers who remain
    Exposed, in spite of this retreat.
A one, his liver's slit straight through;
    Sob and saliva down it drain.
The most that modern war can do
    Dulls his complexion in his pain;
While Bud, hysterical because
    His frantic nerve is fit to bust,
Cries: 'Joe. Don't die,' though die he does.
    His slackened lips absorb the dust.

Outside, their other boy friends bleed
    Like murder, while the wilder, they
Work off hot rage or terror, shed
    Layers of self, like skins, away.
Here's a commencement to a show
    Of selfless love we all might spread
From common friend to common foe,
    Sparing our livers from their lead.

Till then, though, I shall bear my brunt,
    Cursing the colonel from my Rear;
Lavishly let lads Up Front
    Spend all their love, share all my fear.

ALUN LEWIS

Christmas Holiday

Big-uddered piebald cattle low;
The shivering chestnut stallion dozes;
The fat wife sighs in her chair,
Her lap is filled with paper roses;
The poacher sleeps in the goose-girl's arms;
Incurious after so much eating
All human beings are replete.

But the cock upon the dunghill feels
God's needle quiver in his brain
And thrice he crows; and at the sound
The sober and the tipsy men
Jump out of bed with one accord
And start the war again.

The fat wife comfortably sleeping
Sighs and licks her lips and smiles.

But the goose-girl is weeping.

Horror:
'Father, I Dread this Air'

DAVID GASCOYNE

The Uncertain Battle

Away the horde rode, in a storm of hail
And steel-blue lightning. Hurtled by the wind
Into their eardrums from behind the hill
Came in increasing bursts the startled sound
Of trumpets in the unseen hostile camp. –
Down through a raw black hole in heaven stared
The horror-blanched moon's eye. Across the swamp
Five ravens flapped; and the storm disappeared
Soon afterwards, like them, into that pit
Of Silence which lies waiting to consume
Even the braggart World itself at last . . .
The candle in the hermit's cave burned out
At dawn, as usual. – No-one ever came
Back down the hill, to say which side had lost.

LOUIS SIMPSON

The Battle

Helmet and rifle, pack and overcoat
Marched through a forest. Somewhere up ahead
Guns thudded. Like the circle of a throat
The night on every side was turning red.

They halted and they dug. They sank like moles
Into the clammy earth between the trees.
And soon the sentries, standing in their holes,
Felt the first snow. Their feet began to freeze.

At dawn the first shell landed with a crack.
Then shells and bullets swept the icy woods.
This lasted many days. The snow was black.
The corpses stiffened in their scarlet hoods.

Most clearly of that battle I remember
The tiredness in eyes, how hands looked thin
Around a cigarette, and the bright ember
Would pulse with all the life there was within.

C. DAY LEWIS

Reconciliation

All day beside the shattered tank he'd lain
Like a limp creature hacked out of its shell,
Now shrivelling on the desert's grid,
Now floating above a sharp-set ridge of pain.

There came a roar, like water, in his ear.
The mortal dust was laid. He seemed to be lying
In a cool coffin of stone walls,
While memory slid towards a plunging weir.

The time that was, the time that might have been,
Find in this shell of stone a chance to kiss
Before they part eternally:
He feels a world without, a world within

Wrestle like old antagonists, until each is
Balancing each. Then, in a heavenly calm,
The lock gates open, and beyond
Appear the argent, swan-assemblied reaches.

KEITH DOUGLAS

Vergissmeinicht

Three weeks gone and the combatants gone,
returning over the nightmare ground
we found the place again, and found
the soldier sprawling in the sun.

The frowning barrel of his gun
overshadowing. As we came on
that day, he hit my tank with one
like the entry of a demon.

Look. Here is the gunpit spoil
the dishonoured picture of his girl
who has put: *Steffi. Vergissmeinicht*
in a copybook gothic script.

We see him almost with content
abased, and seeming to have paid
and mocked at by his own equipment
that's hard and good when he's decayed.

But she would weep to see to-day
how on his skin the swart flies move;
the dust upon the paper eye
and the burst stomach like a cave.

For here the lover and killer are mingled
who had one body and one heart.
And death who had the soldier singled
has done the lover mortal hurt.

BERNARD GUTTERIDGE

The Enemy Dead

The dead are always searched.
It's not a man, the blood-soaked
Mess of rice and flesh and bones
Whose pockets you flip open;
And these belongings are only
The counterpart to scattered ball
Or the abandoned rifle.

Yet later the man lives.
His postcard of a light blue

Donkey and sandy minarets
Reveals a man at last.
'Object – the panther mountains!
Two – a tired soldier of Kiku!
Three – my sister the bamboo sigh!'

Then again the man dies.
And only what he has seen
And felt, loved and feared
Stays as a hill, a soldier, a girl:
Are printed in the skeleton
Whose white bones divide and float away
Like nervous birds in the sky.

CHARLES CAUSLEY

Song of the Dying Gunner A.A.1

Oh mother my mouth is full of stars
As cartridges in the tray
My blood is a twin-branched scarlet tree
And it runs all runs away.

Oh *Cooks to the Galley* is sounded off
And the lads are down in the mess
But I lie done by the forrard gun
With a bullet in my breast.

Don't send me a parcel at Christmas time
Of socks and nutty and wine
And don't depend on a long weekend
By the Great Western Railway line.

Farewell, Aggie Weston, the Barracks at Guz,
Hang my tiddley suit on the door
I'm sewn up neat in a canvas sheet
And I shan't be home no more.

LINCOLN KIRSTEIN

Foresight

Previsioning death in advance, our doom is delayed.
I guess mine:
I'm driving for some dumb officer on this raid:

I can't doubt his sense of direction, his perfect right.
Still, he's wrong.
I hint we're too far front. Been warned plenty about this before.

Base far off. No lights may be shown. He starts to get sore.
Lost, our road.
He feels he's failed. Abruptly down drops night.

Anticipate panic: his, mine, contagions fear takes.
THIS IS IT.
Not good. I invoke calm plus prayer for both our sakes.

Calm makes sense. Prayer is less useful than gin or a smoke.
Where are we?
If this ass hadn't tried to crack his great big joke,

Pushing beyond where he knew well we were told to go,
We'd be safe.
Checking my estimate, my unvoiced I Told You So,

Granite bang-bangs blossom all over hell and gone.
Let me Out!
My foreseen fright swells, a warm swarm and we're sure done

In by Mistake, including his fright, faking him brave;
Me the same,
Making me clam tight when I oughta had the brains to save

Our skins, sparing official pride by baring my fear:
(Please, sir. Turn.)
Sharing his shame with me, who, also, deserve some. Oh dear,

It's too late. The end of two nervous careers,
Of dear me,
And him, dear doubtless to someone, worth her dear tears.

RANDALL JARRELL

The Death of the Ball Turret Gunner

From my mother's sleep I fell into the State,
And I hunched in its belly till my wet fur froze.
Six miles from earth, loosed from its dream of life,
I woke to black flak and the nightmare fighters.
When I died they washed me out of the turret with a hose.

JOHN BAYLISS

Reported Missing

With broken wing they limped across the sky
caught in late sunlight, with their gunner dead,
one engine gone, – the type was out of date, –
blood on the fuselage turning brown from red.

Knew it was finished, looking at the sea
which shone back patterns in kaleidoscope,
knew that their shadow would meet them by the way,
close and catch at them, drown their single hope.

Sat in this tattered scarecrow of the sky,
hearing it cough, the great plane catching
now the first dark clouds upon its wing-base,
patching the straight tear in evening mockery:

So two men waited, saw the third dead face,
and wondered when the wind would let them die.

RANDALL JARRELL

A Pilot from the Carrier

Strapped at the center of the blazing wheel,
His flesh ice-white against the shattered mask,
He tears at the easy clasp, his sobbing breaths
Misting the fresh blood lightening to flame,
Darkening to smoke; trapped there in pain
And fire and breathlessness, he struggles free
Into the sunlight of the upper sky –
And falls, a quiet bundle in the sky,
The miles to warmth, to air, to waking:
To the great flowering of his life, the hemisphere
That holds his dangling years. In its long slow sway
The world steadies and is almost still . . .
He is alone; and hangs in knowledge
Slight, separate, estranged: a lonely eye
Reading a child's first scrawl, the carrier's wake –
The travelling milk-like circle of a miss
Beside the plant-like genius of the smoke
That shades, on the little deck, the little blaze
Toy-like as the glitter of the wing-guns,
Shining as the fragile sun-marked plane
That grows to him, rubbed silver tipped with flame.

HAMISH HENDERSON

We Show You That Death as a Dancer

For Captain Ian McLeod

Death the dancer poked his skull
Into our drawing-room furtively
Before a bullet cracked the lull
And stripped jack-bare the rowan tree
Now flesh drops off from every part
And in his dance he shows his art.

The fundamental now appears,
The ultimate stockade of bone.
He'll neutralize the coward years
And all poor flesh's ills condone.
When we lie stickit in the sand
He'll dance into his promised land.

Alamein, 1942.

DYLAN THOMAS

A Refusal to Mourn the Death, by Fire, of a Child in London

Never until the mankind making
Bird beast and flower
Father and all humbling darkness
Tells silence the last light breaking
And the still hour
Is come of the sea tumbling in harness

And I must enter again the round
Zion of the water bead
And the synagogue of the ear of corn
Shall I let pray the shadow of a sound
Or sow my salt seed
In the least valley of sackcloth to mourn

The majesty and burning of the child's death.
I shall not murder
The mankind of her going with a grave truth
Nor blaspheme down the stations of the breath
With any further
Elegy of innocence and youth.

Deep with the first dead lies London's daughter,
Robed in the long friends,
The grains beyond age, the dark veins of her mother,
Secret by the unmourning water
Of the riding Thames.
After the first death, there is no other.

ALUN LEWIS

Easter in Christmas

What dark and terrible shadow is swaying in the wind?

Beautiful are thy dwellings, Lord of Hosts,
The choir-boys in white go softly singing;
The world is full of pale frustrated ghosts.

Lovers cannot reach each other;
Stars are burnt by an insane fire;
The night is red and loud; the choir-boys
Sing softly ghostly vespers of desire.

What dark and terrible shadow is swaying in the wind?

An agitator and two thieves are swaying in the wind.

The End of War
and the Limit of Poetry:
'The Fate of Our Provincial Star'

ROY FULLER

Autumn 1942

Season of rains: the horizon like an illness
Daily retreating and advancing: men
Swarming on aircraft: things that leave their den
And prowl the suburbs: cries in the starlit stillness –

Into the times' confusion such sharp captions
Are swiftly cut, as symbols give themselves
To poets, though the convenient nymphs and elves
They know fall sadly short of their conceptions.

I see giraffes that lope, half snake, half steed,
A slowed-up film; the soft bright zebra race,
Unreal as rocking horses; and the face –
A solemn mandarin's – of the wildebeest.

And sometimes in the mess the men and their
Pathetic personal trash become detached
From what they move on; and my days are patched
With newspapers about the siege-like war.

Should I be asked to speak the truth, these are
What I should try to explain, and leave unsaid
Our legacy of failure from the dead.
The silent fate of our provincial star.

But what can be explained? The animals
Are what you make of them, are words, are visions,
And they for us are moving in dimensions
Impertinent to use or watch at all.

And of the men there's nothing to be said:
Only events, with which they wrestle, can
Transfigure them or make them other than
Things to be loved or hated and soon dead.

It is the news at which I hesitate,
That glares authentically between the bars
Of style and lies, and holds enough of fears
And history, and is not too remote.

And tells me that the age is thus: chokes back
My private suffering, the ghosts of nature
And of the mind: it says the human features
Are mutilated, have a dreadful lack.

It half convinces me that some great faculty,
Like hands, has been eternally lost and all
Our virtues now are the high and horrible
Ones of a streaming wound which heals in evil.

RICHARD EBERHART

The Fury of Aerial Bombardment

You would think the fury of aerial bombardment
Would rouse God to relent; the infinite spaces
Are still silent. He looks on shock-pried faces.
History, even, does not know what is meant.

You would feel that after so many centuries
God would give man to repent; yet he can kill
As Cain could, but with multitudinous will,
No farther advanced than in his ancient furies.

Was man made stupid to see his own stupidity?
Is God by definition indifferent, beyond us all?
Is the eternal truth man's fighting soul
Wherein the Beast ravens in its own avidity?

Of Van Wettering I speak, and Averill,
Names on a list, whose faces I do not recall
But they are gone to early death, who late in school
Distinguished the belt feed lever from the belt holding pawl.

CHARLES CAUSLEY

Conversation in Gibraltar 1943

We sit here, talking of Barea and Lorca
Meeting the iron eye of the Spanish clock.
We have cut, with steel bows, the jungle of salt-water,
Sustaining the variable sea-fevers of home and women,
To walk the blazing ravine
Of the profitable Rock.

We hold, in our pockets, no comfortable return tickets:
Only the future, gaping like some hideous fable.

The antique Mediterranean of history and Alexander,
The rattling galley and the young Greek captains
Are swept up and piled
Under the table.

We have walked to Europa and looked east to the invisible island,
The bitter rock biting the heel through the shoe-leather.
Rain's vague infantry, the Levant, parachutes on the stone lion
And soon, soon, under our feet and the thin steel deck
We shall be conscious of miles of perpendicular sea,
And the Admiralty weather.

HOWARD NEMEROV

Redeployment

They say the war is over. But water still
Comes bloody from the taps, and my pet cat
In his disorder vomits worms which crawl
Swiftly away. Maybe they leave the house.
These worms are white, and flecked with the cat's blood.

The war may be over. I know a man
Who keeps a pleasant souvenir, he keeps
A soldier's dead blue eyeballs that he found
Somewhere – hard as chalk, and blue as slate.
He clicks them in his pocket while he talks.

And now there are cockroaches in the house,
They get slightly drunk on DDT,
Are fast, hard, shifty – can be drowned but not
Without you hold them under quite some time.
People say the Mexican kind can fly.

The end of the war. I took it quietly
Enough. I tried to wash the dirt out of
My hair and from under my fingernails,
I dressed in clean white clothes and went to bed.
I heard the dust falling between the walls.

RICHARD EBERHART

from Brotherhood of Men

Rumors of liberation. We could not believe it.
Liberation came. Planes came over parachuting
Packages. One plummeted through a sky-light,
Broke one of our legs. Greedy as children,
We ate chocolate until we were sick,
Suspect bellies could not stand it.
It would take us years to get well,
Our bones soft and easily breakable.
My hand broke, opening the door of a car.

Rings I have, watches, tokens, a dog tag
To take back to the land of the living,
From the dead to deliver to fathers or sisters,
Cherished possessions of my luckless companions
Lost in four years of rooted abuse.
O to forget, forget the fever and famine,
The fierceness of visions, the faith beyond reason,
To forget man's lot in the folly of man.
And swear never to kill a living being,
To live for love, the lost country of man's longing.

And yet I know (a knowledge unspeakable)
That we were at our peak when in the depths,
Lived close to life when cuffed by death,
Had visions of brotherhood when we were broken,
Learned compassion beyond the curse of passion,
And never in after years those left to live
Would treat with truth as in those savage times,
And sometimes wish that they had died
As did those many crying in their arms.

KEITH DOUGLAS

from The Offensive

The stars dead heroes in the sky
may well approve the way you die
nor will the sun
revile those who survive because
for the dying and promising there was
these evils remain:

when you are dead and the harm done
the orators and clerks go on
the rulers of interims and wars
effete and stable as stars.

The stars in their fragile house
are the heavenly symbols of a class
dead in their seats,
and the officious sun goes round
organising life; and what he's planned
Time comes and eats.

The sun goes round and the stars go round
the nature of eternity is circular
and man must spend his life to find
all our successes and failures are similar.

RANDALL JARRELL

The Range in the Desert

Where the lizard ran to its little prey
And a man on a horse rode by in a day
They set their hangars: a continent
Taught its conscripts its unloved intent
In the scrawled fire, the singing lead –

Protocols of the quick and dead.
The wounded gunner, his missions done,
Fired absently in the range's sun;
And, chained with cartridges, the clerk
Sat sweating at his war-time work.
The cold flights bombed – again, again –
The craters of the lunar plain . . .

All this was priceless: men were paid
For these rehearsals of the raids
That used up cities at a rate
That left the coals without a State
To call another's; till the worse
Ceded at last, without remorse,
Their conquests to their conquerors.
The equations were without two powers.

Profits and death grow marginal:
Only the mourning and the mourned recall
The wars we lose, the wars we win;
And the world is – what it has been.

The lizard's tongue licks angrily
The shattered membranes of the fly.

ALUN LEWIS

To Edward Thomas

(On visiting the memorial stone above Steep in Hampshire)

1

On the way up from Sheet I met some children
Filling a pram with brushwood; higher still
Beside Steep church an old man pointed out
A rough white stone upon a flinty spur
Projecting from the high autumnal woods . . .
I doubt if much has changed since you came here
On your last leave; except the stone; it bears
Your name and trade: 'To Edward Thomas, Poet'.

2

Climbing the steep path through the copse I knew
My cares weighed heavily as yours, my gift
Much less, my hope
No more than yours.
And like you I felt sensitive and somehow apart,
Lonely and exalted by the friendship of the wind
And the placid afternoon enfolding
The dangerous future and the smile.

3

I sat and watched the dusky berried ridge
Of yew-trees, deepened by oblique dark shafts,
Throw back the flame of red and gold and russet
That leapt from beech and ash to birch and chestnut
Along the downward arc of the hill's shoulder,
And sunlight with discerning fingers
Softly explore the distant wooded acres,
Touching the farmsteads one by one with lightness
Until it reached the Downs, whose soft green pastures
Went slanting sea- and skywards to the limits
Where sight surrenders and the mind alone
Can find the sheep's tracks and the grazing.

And for that moment Life appeared
As gentle as the view I gazed upon.

4

Later, a whole day later, I remembered
This war and yours and your weary
Circle of failure and your striving
To make articulate the groping voices
Of snow and rain and dripping branches
And love that ailing in itself cried out
About the straggling eaves and ringed the candle
With shadows slouching round your buried head;
And in the lonely house there was no ease
For you, or Helen, or those small perplexed
Children of yours who only wished to please.

Divining this, I knew the voice that called you
Was soft and neutral as the sky
Breathing on the grey horizon, stronger
Than night's immediate grasp, the limbs of mercy
Oblivious as the blood; and growing clearer,
More urgent as all else dissolved away,
– Projected books, half-thoughts, the children's
     birthdays,
And wedding anniversaries as cold
As dates in history – the dream
Emerging from the fact that folds a dream,
The endless rides of stormy-branchèd dark
Whose fibres are a thread within the hand –

Till suddenly, at Arras, you possessed that hinted land.

SIDNEY KEYES

Europe's Prisoners

Never a day, never a day passes
But I remember them, their stoneblind faces
Beaten by arclights, their eyes turned inward
Seeking an answer and their passage homeward:

For being citizens of time, they never
Would learn the body's nationality.
Tortured for years now, they refuse to sever
Spirit from flesh or accept our callow century.

Not without hope, but lacking present solace,
The preacher knows the feel of nails and grace;
The singer snores; the orator's facile hands
Are fixed in a gesture no one understands.

Others escaped, yet paid for their betrayal:
Even the politicians with their stale
Visions and cheap flirtation with the past
Will not die any easier at the last.

The ones who took to garrets and consumption
In foreign cities, found a deeper dungeon
Than any Dachau. Free but still confined
The human lack of pity split their mind.

Whatever days, whatever seasons pass,
The prisoners must stare in pain's white face:
Until at last the courage they have learned
Shall burst the walls and overturn the world.

STEPHEN SPENDER

Ultima Ratio Regum

The guns spell money's ultimate reason
In letters of lead on the Spring hillside.
But the boy lying dead under the olive trees
Was too young and too silly
To have been notable to their important eye.
He was a better target for a kiss.

When he lived, tall factory hooters never summoned him
Nor did restaurant plate-glass doors revolve to wave him in.
His name never appeared in the papers.
The world maintained its traditional wall
Round the dead with their gold sunk deep as a well,
Whilst his life, intangible as a Stock Exchange rumour, drifted
      outside.

O too lightly he threw down his cap
One day when the breeze threw petals from the trees.
The unflowering wall sprouted with guns,
Machine-gun anger quickly scythed the grasses;
Flags and leaves fell from hands and branches;
The tweed cap rotted in the nettles.

Consider his life which was valueless
In terms of employment, hotel ledgers, news files.
Consider. One bullet in ten thousand kills a man.
Ask. Was so much expenditure justified
On the death of one so young, and so silly
Lying under the olive trees, O world, O death?

SIDNEY KEYES

War Poet

I am the man who looked for peace and found
My own eyes barbed.
I am the man who groped for words and found
An arrow in my hand.
I am the builder whose firm walls surround
A slipping land.
When I grow sick or mad
Mock me not nor chain me:
When I reach for the wind
Cast me not down:
Though my face is a burnt book
And a wasted town.

EDWIN MUIR

The Child Dying

Unfriendly friendly universe,
I pack your stars into my purse,
And bid you, bid you so farewell.
That I can leave you, quite go out,
Go out, go out beyond all doubt,
My father says, is the miracle.

You are so great, and I so small:
I am nothing, you are all:
Being nothing, I can take this way.
Oh I need neither rise nor fall,
For when I do not move at all
I shall be out of all your day.

It's said some memory will remain
In the other place, grass in the rain,

Light on the land, sun on the sea,
A flitting grace, a phantom face,
But the world is out. There is no place
Where it and its ghost can ever be.

Father, father, I dread this air
Blown from the far side of despair,
The cold cold corner. What house, what hold,
What hand is there? I look and see
Nothing-filled eternity,
And the great round world grows weak and old.

Hold my hand, oh hold it fast –
I am changing! – until at last
My hand in yours no more will change,
Though yours change on. You here, I there,
So hand in hand, twin-leafed despair –
I did not know death was so strange.

ACKNOWLEDGEMENTS

The publisher has made every effort to contact the copyright holder of each poem but wishes to apologise to those he has been unable to trace. Grateful acknowledgement is made for permission to reprint the poems on the following pages:

15. 'next to of course god america i' is reprinted from IS 5 poems by E.E. Cummings, edited by George James Firmage, by permission of Liveright Publishing Corporation (US rights). Reprinted from *Complete Poems* by permission of Grafton Books, a division of the Collins Publishing Group (UK rights). Copyright © 1985 by E.E. Cummings Trust. Copyright 1926 by Horace Liveright. Copyright © 1954 by E.E. Cummings. Copyright © 1985 by George James Firmage.

16. 'The Soldier Addresses his Body' by Edgell Rickword. Reprinted from *Behind the Eyes* (1976) by permission of Carcanet Press Limited.

20. 'Winter Warfare' by Edgell Rickword. Reprinted from *Behind the Eyes* (1976) by permission of Carcanet Press Limited.

26. 'The Rear-Guard' by Siegfried Sassoon. Reprinted by permission of George T. Sassoon.

27. 'Counter-Attack' by Siegfried Sassoon. Reprinted by permission of George T. Sassoon.

29. 'A Pot of Tea' by Robert Service. Reprinted by permission of Feinman and Krasilovsky. P.C. (UK rights) and by permission of The Putnam Publishing Group from *The Collected Poems of Robert Service* by Robert Service. Copyright © 1940 by G.P. Putnam's Sons (US rights).

30. 'My Company' by Herbert Read. Reprinted from *Collected Poems* by permission of Faber & Faber.

38. 'Motley' by Walter de la Mare. Reprinted by permission of The Literary Trustees of Walter de la Mare and The Society of Authors as their representative.

49. 'Moonrise over Battlefield' by Edgell Rickword. Reprinted from *Behind the Eyes* (1976) by permission of Carcanet Press Limited.

57. 'i sing of Olaf glad and big' is reprinted from *Viva*, poems by E.E. Cummings, edited by George James Firmage, by permission of Liveright Publishing Corporation (US rights). Reprinted from *Complete Poems* by permission of Grafton Books, a division of the Collins Publishing Group (UK rights). Copyright © 1931, 1959 by E.E. Cummings. Copyright © 1979, 1973 by the Trustees for the E.E. Cummings Trust. Copyright © 1979, 1973 by George James Firmage.

58. 'Suicide in the Trenches' by Siegfried Sassoon. Reprinted by permission of George T. Sassoon.

59. 'Untitled' by A.P. Herbert. Reprinted by permission of A.P. Watt Limited on behalf of Crystal Hale and Jocelyn Herbert.

62. 'Dead Cow Farm' by Robert Graves reprinted from *Poems of War* by permission of A.P. Watt Limited on behalf of the Executors of the Estate of Robert Graves.

71. 'Does it Matter?' by Siegfried Sassoon. Reprinted by permission of George T. Sassoon.

71. From 'How Shall we Rise to Greet the Dawn?' by Osbert Sitwell. Reprinted from *Selected Poems* by permission of the Duckworth Group.

75. 'Memorial Tablet' by Siegfried Sassoon. Reprinted by permission of George T. Sassoon.

75. "Blighters" by Siegfried Sassoon. Reprinted by permission of George T. Sassoon.

86. 'The Forest of the Dead' by J. Griffyth Fairfax. Reprinted from *Mesopotamia* by permission of John Murray (Publishers) Ltd.

90. 'On Passing the New Menin Gate' by Siegfried Sassoon. Reprinted by permission of George T. Sassoon.

93. 'That Exploit of Yours' by Ford Madox Ford reprinted by permission of the Estate of Ford Madox Ford from *The Bodley Head Ford Madox Ford* published by The Bodley Head.

93. 'Recalling War' by Robert Graves reprinted from *Poems of War* by permission of A.P. Watt Limited on behalf of the Executors of the Estate of Robert Graves.

95. 'Aftermath' by Siegfried Sassoon. Reprinted by permission of George T. Sassoon.

98. 'Hugh Selwyn Mauberly' (IV and V). Reprinted from Ezra Pound: *Personae*. Copyright 1926 by Ezra Pound. Reprinted by permission of New Directions Publishing Corporation (US rights). Reprinted by permission of Faber and Faber Ltd from *Collected Shorter Poems* by Ezra Pound (UK rights).

102. 'The Next War' by Osbert Sitwell. Reprinted from *Selected Poems* by permission of the Duckworth Group.

104. 'In September 1939' by Bernard Gutteridge. Reprinted from *Traveller's Eye* by permission of Routledge.

105. 'Six Young Men' by Ted Hughes. Reprinted by permission of Faber and Faber Ltd from *The Hawk in the Rain* by Ted Hughes.

106. 'Autumn, 1939' by Alun Lewis. Extract taken from *Raider's Dawn* (1942) by Alun Lewis, reproduced by kind permission of Unwin Hyman Ltd.

107. 'To a Conscript of 1940' by Herbert Read, reprinted from *A War within a War* by permission of Faber and Faber Ltd.

110. 'Death is a Matter of Mathematics' by Barry Amiel, reprinted from *Poems from India, by Members of the Forces* edited by R.N. Currey and R.V. Gibson, Oxford University Press, Bombay 1945, London 1946.

111. 'Judging Distances' from 'Lessons of the War' by Henry Reed. Reprinted from *A Map of Verona* by permission of the Literary Executor of the Estate of Henry Reed.

113. 'Destroyers in the Arctic' by Alan Ross, reprinted from *Blindfold Games* (Collins Harvill, 1986) by permission of the author.

114. 'The Bofors AA Gun' by Gavin Ewart, reprinted from *Collected Poems* by permission of Century Hutchinson Ltd.

115. 'A Front' reprinted by permission of Faber and Faber Ltd from *The Complete Poems* by Randall Jarrell (UK rights). Reprinted from *The Complete Poems* by Randall Jarrell. Copyright © 1944 by Mrs Randall Jarrell. Copyright renewed 1971 by Mrs Randall Jarrell. Reprinted by permission of Farrar, Straus and Giroux, Inc. (US rights).

115. 'Unseen Fire' by R.N. Currey. Reprinted from *This Other Planet* by permission of Routledge.

116. 'Dam Neck, Virginia' by Richard Eberhart reprinted from *Collected Poems 1930–1960* (Chatto & Windus 1960) by permission of the author, with acknowledgements to Oxford Unversity Press, New York.

117. 'How to Kill' by Keith Douglas. Copyright © Marie J. Douglas 1978. Reprinted from *The Complete Poems of Keith Douglas* edited by Desmond Graham (1978) by permission of Oxford University Press.

120. 'Advice for a Journey' by Sidney Keyes reprinted from *Collected Poems* by permission of Routledge.

121. 'Infantry' by Alun Lewis. Extract taken from *Ha! Ha! Among the Trumpets* (1945) by Alun Lewis, reproduced by kind permission of Unwin Hyman Ltd.

121. 'The Dead Wingman' by Randall Jarrell. Reprinted by permission of Faber and Faber Ltd from *The Complete Poems* by Randall Jarrell (UK rights). Reprinted from *The Complete Poems* by Randall Jarrell. Copyright © 1945 by Mrs Randall Jarrell. Copyright renewed 1972 by Mrs Randall Jarrell. Reprinted by permission of Farrar, Straus and Giroux, Inc. (US rights).

122. 'Enfidaville' by Keith Douglas. Copyright © Marie J. Douglas 1978. Reprinted from

The Complete Poems of Keith Douglas edited by Desmond Graham (1978) by permission of Oxford University Press.

123. 'A Funeral Oration' by Drummond Allison. Reprinted by permission of Fortune Press/Charles Skilton Ltd.

124. 'De Profundis' by David Gascoyne. Copyright © David Gascoyne 1985, 1988. Reprinted from David Gascoyne's *Collected Poems 1988* (1988) by permission of Oxford University Press.

125. 'At the British War Cemetery, Bayeux' by Charles Causley. Reprinted from *Union Street* by permission of Macmillan.

126. 'Three Pleas' by Henry Treece. Reprinted by permission of John Johnson Limited.

127. 'The Sentry' by Alun Lewis. Extract taken from *Raider's Dawn* (1942) by Alun Lewis, reproduced by kind permission of Unwin Hyman Ltd.

128. 'Song to Hymen: 1942' by Anthony Richardson. Reprinted by permission of Harrap Limited.

129. 'The Middle of a War' by Roy Fuller. Reprinted by permission of Martin Secker & Warburg Limited. Copyright © Roy Fuller 1985.

132. 'P.O.E.' by Lincoln Kirstein. Reprinted by permission of the author.

133. 'In Africa' by Roy Fuller. Reprinted by permission of Martin Secker & Warburg Limited. Copyright © Roy Fuller 1985.

133. 'The Peasants' by Alun Lewis. Extract taken from *Ha! Ha! Among the Trumpets* (1945) by Alun Lewis, reproduced by kind permission of Unwin Hyman Ltd.

134. 'Burial Flags' by R.N. Currey. Reprinted from *Indian Landscape* by permission of Routledge.

135. 'Cairo Jag' by Keith Douglas. Copyright © Marie J. Douglas 1978. Reprinted from *The Complete Poems of Keith Douglas* edited by Desmond Graham (1978) by permission of Oxford University Press.

136. 'A Camp in the Prussian Forest' by Randall Jarrell. Reprinted by permission of Faber and Faber Ltd from *The Complete Poems* by Randall Jarrell (UK rights). Reprinted from *The Complete Poems* by Randall Jarrell copyright © 1946 by Mrs Randall Jarrell. Copyright renewed 1973 by Mrs Randall Jarrell. Reprinted by permission of Farrar, Straus and Giroux, Inc. (US rights).

139. 'End of a Campaign' by Hamish Henderson. Reprinted by permission of the author.

140. 'The Mahratta Ghats' by Alun Lewis. Extract taken from *Ha! Ha! Among the Trumpets* (1945) by Alun Lewis, reproduced by kind permission of Unwin Hyman Ltd.

141. 'Shillong' by Bernard Gutteridge. Reprinted from *Traveller's Eye* by permission of Routledge.

142. 'The Wilderness' by Sidney Keyes. Reprinted from *Collected Poems* by permission of Routledge.

144. 'Embarkation, 1942' by John Jarmain. Reprinted from *Poems* by permission of Collins.

145. 'The Interrrogation' by Edwin Muir. Reprinted by permission of Faber and Faber Ltd from *The Collected Poems of Edwin Muir*.

145. 'The Expected Guest' by Sidney Keyes. Reprinted from *Collected Poems* by permission of Routledge.

147. 'Goodbye' by Alun Lewis. Extract taken from *Ha! Ha! Among the Trumpets* (1945) by Alun Lewis, reproduced by kind permission of Unwin Hyman Ltd.

148. 'Eighth Air Force' by Randall Jarrell. Reprinted by permission of Faber and Faber Ltd from *The Complete Poems* by Randall Jarrell (UK rights). Reprinted from *The Complete Poems* by Randall Jarrell. Copyright © 1947 by Mrs Randall Jarrell. Copyright renewed 1969 by Mrs Randall Jarrell. Reprinted by permission of Farrar, Straus and Giroux, Inc. (US rights).

149. 'What is Terrible' by Roy Fuller. Reprinted by permission of Martin Secker & Warburg Limited. Copyright © Roy Fuller 1985.

Poems 1930–1960 (Chatto and Windus, 1960) by permission of the author, with acknowledgements to Oxford University Press, New York.

172. 'Conversation in Gibraltar 1943' by Charles Causley. Reprinted from Union Street by permission of Macmillan.

173. 'Redeployment' by Howard Nemerov. Reprinted from The Collected Poems of Howard Nemerov, the University of Chicago Press, 1977, reprinted by permission of the author.

174. From 'Brotherhood of Men' by Richard Eberhart. Reprinted from Collected Poems 1930–1960 (Chatto and Windus, 1960) by permission of the author, with acknowledgements to Oxford University Press, New York.

175. From 'The Offensive' by Keith Douglas. Copyright © Marie J. Douglas 1978. Reprinted from The Complete Poems of Keith Douglas edited by Desmond Graham (1978) by permission of Oxford University Press.

175. 'The Range in the Desert' by Randall Jarrell. Reprinted by permission of Faber and Faber Ltd from The Complete Poems by Randall Jarrell (UK rights). Reprinted from The Complete Poems by Randall Jarrell. Copyright © 1947 by Mrs Randall Jarrell. Copyright renewed 1974 by Mrs Randall Jarrell. Reprinted by permission of Farrar, Straus and Giroux, Inc. (US rights).

177. 'To Edward Thomas' by Alun Lewis. Extract taken from Raider's Dawn (1942) by Alun Lewis, reproduced by kind permission of Unwin Hyman Ltd.

179. 'Europe's Prisoners' by Sidney Keyes. Reprinted from Collected Poems by permission of Routledge.

180. 'Ultima Ratio Regum' by Stephen Spender. Reprinted by permission of Faber and Faber Ltd from Collected Poems by Stephen Spender (UK rights). Reprinted from Poems 1934–42, by Stephen Spender, by permission of Random House, Inc. Copyright 1942 and renewed 1970 by Stephen Spender. (US rights).

181. 'War Poet' by Sidney Keyes. Reprinted from Collected Poems by permission of Routledge.

181. 'The Child Dying' by Edwin Muir. Reprinted by permission of Faber and Faber Ltd from The Collected Poems of Edwin Muir.

ILLUSTRATION ACKNOWLEDGEMENTS

The following illustrations are reproduced by courtesy of the Trustees of the Imperial War Museum, London;

Page 112: 'Parade Ground' by Anthony Gross.
Page 124: 'Battle Camp' by Miles Chance.
Page 128: 'Partisan Camp' by H. Hallstone.
Page 146: 'Pilots' by Mervyn Peake.
Page 151: 'TOC H workers' by H. Hallstone.
Page 165: 'Pilot' by Mervyn Peake.
Page 171: 'Bombing up' by Anthony Gross.
Page 176: 'NZ Battery' by Anthony Gross.

INDEX OF FIRST LINES

INDEX OF AUTHORS